MongoDB
Simply In Depth

AJIT SINGH
SULTAN AHMAD

CRUD OPERATION
2DSPHERE INDEX, AGGREGATION
CONNECTIVITY-JAVA, PYTHON & PHP
SHARDING ENVIRONMENT SETUP
AUTHENTICATION, BACKUP, GRIDFS

(c) Copyright 2019, Ajit Singh

Mongodb Simply In Depth

Copyrighted Material

Copyright © 2019 by Ajit Singh. All Rights Reserved.
No part of this publication may be reproduced, stored in a retrieval system or transmitted, in any form or by any means electronic, mechanical, photocopying, recording or otherwise without prior written permission from the author, except for the inclusion of brief quotations in a review.
For information about this title or to order other books and/or electronic media, contact the publisher:

Ajit Singh & Sultan Ahmad
ajit_singh24@yahoo.com
http://www.ajitvoice.in

About Author

Ajit Singh
UGC NET - Assistant Professor
Department of Computer Application
Patna Women's College, Patna, Bihar.

World Record Tittle(s):
1. Online World Record (OWR).
2. Future Kalams Book Of Records.

A PhD candidate at Patliputra University, Bihar, IND working on **"Social Media Predictive Data Analytics"** at the A. N. College Research Centre, Patna, IND. He also holds M.Phil. Degree in Computer Science, and is a Microsoft's MCSE / MCDBA / MCSD.

20+ Years of strong teaching experience for Under Graduate and Post Graduate courses of Computer Science across several colleges of Patna University and NIT Patna, Bihar, IND.

[Contact]
URL: http://www.ajitvoice.in
Email: ajit_singh24@yahoo.com
Ph: +91-923-46-11498

[Memberships]
1. InternetSociety (2168607) - Delhi/Trivendrum Chapters
2. IEEE (95539159)
3. International Association of Engineers (IAENG-233408)
4. Eurasia Research STRA-M19371
5. ORCID https://orcid.org/0000-0002-6093-3457
6. Python Software Foundation
7. Data Science Association
8. Non Fiction Authors Association (NFAA-21979)

I would like to thank my mom, Late Smt. Shakuntala Devi and my wife Mrs Rajyashree Singh for all their blessings and support......
I would also like to thank my elder brother Er Ranbir Singh who gave me the opportunity to start my career in the world of authoring......

Contents

Chapter 1: Introduction & Getting started with MongoDB   5

Section 1.1: Execution of a JavaScript file in MongoDB
Section 1.2: Making the output of find readable in shell
Section 1.3: Complementary Terms
Section 1.4: Installation
Section 1.5: Basic commands on mongo shell
Section 1.6: Hello World

Chapter 2: CRUD Operation
DataBase & Collection   23
Section 2.1: Create
Section 2.2: Update
Section 2.5: Update of embedded documents
Section 2.6: More update operators
Section 2.7: "multi" Parameter while updating multiple documents

Chapter 3: Querying for Data (Getting Started)   29
Section 3.1: Find()
Section 3.2: FindOne()
Section 3.3: limit, skip, sort and count the results of the find() method
Section 3.4: Query Document – Using AND, OR and IN Conditions
Section 3.5: find() method with Projection
Section 3.6: Find() method with Projection
Section 3.7 Update Operators
Section 3.8: $set operator to update specified field(s) in document(s)

Chapter 4: Upserts, Inserts and Collection   33
Section 4.1: Insert a document
Section 4.2: Data Modeling
Section 4.3 Join

Chapter 5: Aggregation   41
Section 5.1: Count
Section 5.2: Sum
Section 5.3: Average
Section 5.4: Operations with arrays
Section 5.5: Aggregate query examples useful for work and learning
Section 5.6: Match
Section 5.7: Get sample data
Section 5.8: Remove docs that have a duplicate field in a collection (dedupe)
Section 5.9: Left Outer Join with aggregation ($Lookup) 30
Section 5.10: Server Aggregation
Section 5.11: Aggregation in a Server Method
Section 5.12: Java and Spring example

Chapter 6: Indexes   48
Section 6.1: Index Creation Basics
Section 6.2: Dropping/Deleting an Index
Section 6.3: Sparse indexes and Partial indexes
Section 6.4: Get Indices of a Collection
Section 6.5: Compound
Section 6.6: Unique Index
Section 6.7: Single field
Section 6.8: Delete
Section 6.9: List
Section 6.10 Map Reduce

Chapter 7: Bulk Operations & 2dsphere Index
Section 7.1: Converting a field to another type and updating the entire collection in Bulk
Section 7.2: 2dsphere Index
Section 7.3: Create a 2dsphere Index

53

Chapter 8: Pluggable Storage Engines
Section 8.1: WiredTiger
Section 8.2: MMAP
Section 8.3: In-memory
Section 8.4: mongo-rocks
Section 8.5: Fusion-io
Section 8.6: TokuMX

56

Chapter 9: Connectivity
Java Driver
Section 9.1: Fetch Collection data with condition
Section 9.2: Create a database user
Section 9.3: Create a tailable cursor

57

Python Driver
Section 9.4: Connect to MongoDB using pymongo
Section 9.5: PyMongo queries
Section 9.6: Update all documents in a collection using PyMongo

PHP Driver
Section 9.7: Connect to MongoDB With PHP

Chapter 10: Mongo as Shards
Section 10.1: Sharding Environment Setup

62

Chapter 11: Replication
Section 11.1: Basic configuration with three nodes
Section 11.2: Mongodb as a Replica Set
Section 11.3: Check MongoDB Replica Set states
Section 11.4: How to configure a ReplicaSet to support TLS/SSL?
Section 11.5: How to connect your Client (Mongo Shell) to a ReplicaSet?

63

Chapter 12: Authentication Mechanisms & Authorization Model in MongoDB
Section 12.1: Authentication Mechanisms

69

Chapter 13: Configuration
Section 13.1: Starting mongo with a specific config file

70

Chapter 14: Backing up and Restoring Data
Section 14.1: Basic mongodump of local default mongod instance
Section 14.2: Basic mongorestore of local default mongod dump
Section 14.3: mongoimport with JSON
Section 14.4: mongoimport with CSV

71

Chapter 15: Upgrading MongoDB version
Section 15.1: Upgrading to 4.0 on Ubuntu 16.04 using apt

73

Chapter 16: MongoDB GridFS, Querying Capped Collection, Sequence

75

Preface

Mongodb is a document-oriented NoSQL database used for high volume data storage. In this free course you will learn how Mongodb can be accessed and its important features like indexing, regular expression, sharding data, etc. Big data can mean big headaches. MongoDB is a document-oriented database designed to be flexible, scalable, and very fast, even with big data loads. It's built for high availability, supports rich, dynamic schemas, and lets you easily distribute data across multiple servers.

This book is a comprehensive guide to MongoDB for application developers. The book begins by explaining what makes MongoDB unique and describing its ideal use cases. A series of chapters designed for MongoDB mastery then leads into detailed examples for leveraging MongoDB in e-commerce, social networking, analytics, and other common applications. Numerous examples will help you develop confidence in the crucial area of data modeling. You'll also love the deep explanations of each feature, including replication, auto-sharding, and deployment.

This book is a comprehensive guide to MongoDB for application developers. The book begins by explaining what makes MongoDB unique and describing it's ideal use cases. A series of chapters designed for MongoDB mastery then leads into detailed examples for leveraging MongoDB in e-commerce, social networking, analytics, and other common applications. Numerous examples will help you develop confidence in the crucial area of data modeling.

This is well-organized book which provides proper explaination you'll need as a student and enough detail to satisfy a developer. Several examples will help you develop confidence in the crucial area of data modeling. You'll also love the deep explanations of each feature, including replication, auto-sharding, and deployment.

The first chapters cover a lot of theory but later you dive into practical hands-on experience setting up and configuring MongoDB from scratch. This is crucial if you want to truly understand the database environment. Later chapters even offer source code from multiple languages like Java, Python, and PHP. This lets you see how applications can scale using Mongo regardless of the backend language. You can learn sharding and replication for scaling databases.

This book is very compact with less than 100 pages. But its also incredibly detailed and wastes no time diving right into the action and ease of use......

What's inside

- NoSQL, Architecture of MongoDB
- Standard DB operations, Indexes, queries
- Map-reduce for custom aggregations and reporting
- Java, Python and PHP Connectivity
- Schema design patterns
- Deploying for scale and high availability

Chapter 1:
Introduction & Getting started with MongoDB

It is often said that technology moves at a blazing pace. It's true that there is an ever growing list of new technologies and techniques being released. However, I've long been of the opinion that the fundamental technologies used by programmers move at a rather slow pace. One could spend years learning little yet remain relevant. What is striking though is the speed at which established technologies get replaced. Seemingly overnight, long-established technologies find themselves threatened by shifts in developer focus.

- MongoDB stores data in flexible, JSON-like documents, meaning fields can vary from document to document and data structure can be changed over time

- The document model maps to the objects in your application code, making data easy to work with

- Ad hoc queries, indexing, and real time aggregation provide powerful ways to access and analyze your data

- MongoDB is a distributed database at its core, so high availability, horizontal scaling, and geographic distribution are built in and easy to use

- MongoDB is free and open-source. Versions released prior to October 16, 2018 are published under the AGPL. All versions released after October 16, 2018, including patch fixes for prior versions, are published under the Server Side PublicLicense (SSPL) v1.

Nothing could be more representative of this sudden shift than the progress of NoSQL technologies against well-established relational databases. It almost seems like one day the web was being driven by a few RDBMSs, and the next, five or so NoSQL solutions had established themselves as worthy solutions.

History of MongoDB

Version	Release Date
4.0.6	Feb'7, 2019
3.4	2016-11-29
3.2	2015-12-08
3.0	2015-03-03
2.6	2014-04-08
2.4	2013-03-19
2.2	2012-08-29
2.0	2011-09-12
1.8	2011-03-16
1.6	2010-08-31
1.4	2010-03-25
1.2	2009-12-10

Even though these transitions seem to happen overnight, the reality is that they can take years to become accepted practice. The initial enthusiasm is driven by a relatively small set of developers and companies. Solutions are refined, lessons learned and seeing that a new technology is here to stay, others slowly try it for themselves. Again, this is particularly true in the case of NoSQL where many solutions aren't replacements for more traditional storage solutions, but rather address a specific need in addition to what one might get from traditional offerings.

Having said all of that, the first thing we ought to do is explain what is meant by NoSQL. It's a broad term that means different things to different people. Personally, I use it very broadly to mean a system that plays a part in the storage of data. Put another way, NoSQL (again, for me), is the belief that your persistence layer isn't necessarily the responsibility of a single system. Where relational database vendors have historically tried to position their software as a one-size-fits-all solution, NoSQL leans towards smaller units of responsibility where the best tool for a given job can be leveraged. So, your NoSQL stack might still leverage a relational database, say MySQL, but it'll also contain Redis as a persistence lookup for specific parts of the system as well as Hadoop for your intensive data processing. Put simply, NoSQL is about being open and aware of alternative, existing and additional patterns and tools for managing your data.

You might be wondering where MongoDB fits into all of this. As a document-oriented database, MongoDB is a more generalized NoSQL solution. It should be viewed as an alternative to relational databases. Like relational databases, it too can benefit from being paired with some of the more specialized NoSQL solutions.

MongoDB Example

The below example shows how a document can be modeled in MongoDB.

1. The _id field is added by MongoDB to uniquely identify the document in the collection.
2. What you can note is that the Order Data (OrderID, Product, and Quantity) which in RDBMS will normally be stored in a separate table, while in MongoDB it is actually stored as an embedded document in the collection itself. This is one of the key differences in how data is modeled in MongoDB.

```
{
    _id : <ObjectId> ,
    CustomerName : Guru99 ,
    Order:
        {
            OrderID: 111         example of
            Product: ProductA    how data can
            Quantity: 5          be embedded
        }                        in a document
}
```

MongoDB Architecture & it's Key Components

Below are a few of the common terms used in MongoDB

1. _id – This is a field required in every MongoDB document. The _id field represents a unique value in the MongoDB document. The _id field is like the document's primary key. If you create a new document without an _id field, MongoDB will automatically create the field. So for example, if we see the example of the above customer table, Mongo DB will add a 24 digit unique identifier to each document in the collection.

_Id	CustomerID	CustomerName	OrderID
563479cc8a8a4246bd27d784	11	Guru99	111
563479cc7a8a4246bd47d784	22	Trevor Smith	222
563479cc9a8a4246bd57d784	33	Nicole	333

2. Collection – This is a grouping of MongoDB documents. A collection is the equivalent of a table which is created in any other RDMS such as Oracle or MS SQL. A collection exists within a single database. As seen from the introduction collections don't enforce any sort of structure.
3. Cursor – This is a pointer to the result set of a query. Clients can iterate through a cursor to retrieve results.
4. Database – This is a container for collections like in RDMS wherein it is a container for tables. Each database gets its own set of files on the file system. A MongoDB server can store multiple databases.
5. Document - A record in a MongoDB collection is basically called a document. The document, in turn, will consist of field name and values.
6. Field - A name-value pair in a document. A document has zero or more fields. Fields are analogous to columns in relational databases.

The following diagram shows an example of Fields with Key value pairs. So in the example below CustomerID and 11 is one of the key value pair's defined in the document.

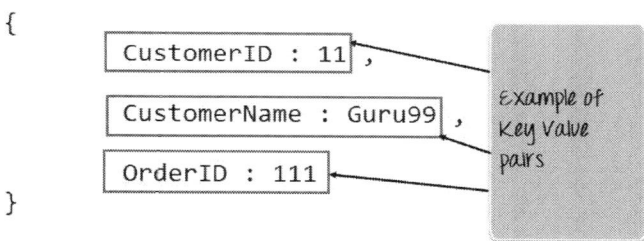

7. JSON – This is known as JavaScript Object Notation. This is a human-readable, plain text format for expressing structured data. JSON is currently supported in many programming languages.

Just a quick note on the key difference between the _id field and a normal collection field. The _id field is used to uniquely identify the documents in a collection and is automatically added by MongoDB when the collection is created.

Why Use MongoDB?

Below are the few of the reasons as to why one should start using MongoDB

1. Document-oriented – Since MongoDB is a NoSQL type database, instead of having data in a relational type format, it stores the data in documents. This makes MongoDB very flexible and adaptable to real business world situation and requirements.
2. Ad hoc queries - MongoDB supports searching by field, range queries, and regular expression searches. Queries can be made to return specific fields within documents.

3. Indexing - Indexes can be created to improve the performance of searches within MongoDB. Any field in a MongoDB document can be indexed.
4. Replication - MongoDB can provide high availability with replica sets. A replica set consists of two or more mongo DB instances. Each replica set member may act in the role of the primary or secondary replica at any time. The primary replica is the main server which interacts with the client and performs all the read/write operations. The Secondary replicas maintain a copy of the data of the primary using built-in replication. When a primary replica fails, the replica set automatically switches over to the secondary and then it becomes the primary server.
5. Load balancing - MongoDB uses the concept of sharding to scale horizontally by splitting data across multiple MongoDB instances. MongoDB can run over multiple servers, balancing the load and/or duplicating data to keep the system up and running in case of hardware failure.

Data Modelling in MongoDB

As we have seen from the Introduction section, the data in MongoDB has a flexible schema. Unlike in SQL databases, where you must have a table's schema declared before inserting data, MongoDB's collections do not enforce document structure. This sort of flexibility is what makes MongoDB so powerful.

When modeling data in Mongo, keep the following things in mind

1. What are the needs of the application – Look at the business needs of the application and see what data and the type of data needed for the application. Based on this, ensure that the structure of the document is decided accordingly.
2. What are data retrieval patterns – If you foresee a heavy query usage then consider the use of indexes in your data model to improve the efficiency of queries.
3. Are frequent insert's, updates and removals happening in the database – Reconsider the use of indexes or incorporate sharding if required in your data modeling design to improve the efficiency of your overall MongoDB environment.

Difference between MongoDB & RDBMS

Below are some of the key term differences between MongoDB and RDBMS

RDBMS	MongoDB	Difference
Table	Collection	In RDBMS, the table contains the columns and rows which are used to store the data whereas, in MongoDB, this same structure is known as a collection. The collection contains documents which in turn contains Fields, which in turn are key-value pairs.
Row	Document	In RDBMS, the row represents a single, implicitly structured data item in a table. In MongoDB, the data is stored in documents.
Column	Field	In RDBMS, the column denotes a set of data values. These in MongoDB are known as Fields.
Joins	Embedded documents	In RDBMS, data is sometimes spread across various tables and in order to show a complete view of all data, a join is sometimes formed across tables to get the data. In MongoDB, the data is normally stored in a single collection, but separated by using Embedded documents. So there is no concept of joins in MongoDB.

Apart from the terms differences, a few other differences are shown below

1. Relational databases are known for enforcing data integrity. This is not an explicit requirement in MongoDB.
2. RDBMS requires that data be normalized first so that it can prevent orphan records and duplicates Normalizing data then has the requirement of more tables, which will then result in more table joins, thus requiring more keys and indexes.

As databases start to grow, performance can start becoming an issue. Again this is not an explicit requirement in MongoDB. MongoDB is flexible and does not need the data to be normalized first.

What is NoSQL?

NoSQL is a non-relational DMS, that does not require a fixed schema, avoids joins, and is easy to scale. NoSQL database is used for distributed data stores with humongous data storage needs. NoSQL is used for Big data and real-time web apps. For example companies like Twitter, Facebook, Google that collect terabytes of user data every single day.

NoSQL database stands for "Not Only SQL" or "Not SQL." Though a better term would NoREL NoSQL caught on. Carl Strozz introduced the NoSQL concept in 1998.

Traditional RDBMS uses SQL syntax to store and retrieve data for further insights. Instead, a NoSQL database system encompasses a wide range of database technologies that can store structured, semi-structured, unstructured and polymorphic data.

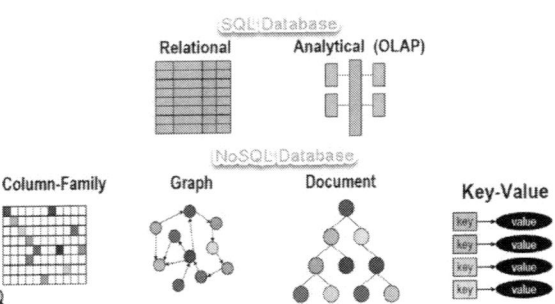

Why NoSQL?

The concept of NoSQL databases became popular with Internet giants like Google, Facebook, Amazon, etc. who deal with huge volumes of data. The system response time becomes slow when you use RDBMS for massive volumes of data.

To resolve this problem, we could "scale up" our systems by upgrading our existing hardware. This process is expensive.

The alternative for this issue is to distribute database load on multiple hosts whenever the load increases. This method is known as "scaling out."

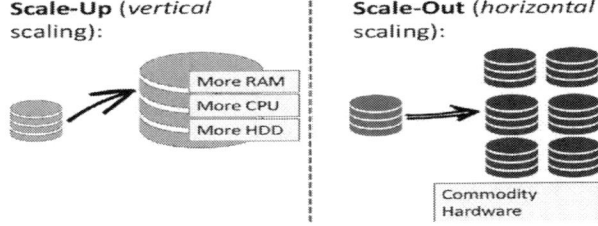

NoSQL database is non-relational, so it scales out better than relational databases as they are designed with web applications in mind.

Brief History of NoSQL Databases

- 1998- Carlo Strozzi use the term NoSQL for his lightweight, open-source relational database
- 2000- Graph database Neo4j is launched
- 2004- Google BigTable is launched
- 2005- CouchDB is launched
- 2007- The research paper on Amazon Dynamo is released
- 2008- Facebooks open sources the Cassandra project
- 2009- The term NoSQL was reintroduced

Features of NoSQL

Non-relational

- NoSQL databases never follow the relational model
- Never provide tables with flat fixed-column records
- Work with self-contained aggregates or BLOBs
- Doesn't require object-relational mapping and data normalization
- No complex features like query languages, query planners, referential integrity joins, ACID

Schema-free

- NoSQL databases are either schema-free or have relaxed schemas
- Do not require any sort of definition of the schema of the data
- Offers heterogeneous structures of data in the same domain

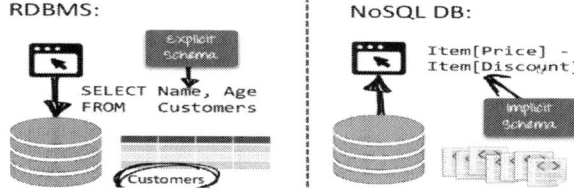

NoSQL is Schema-Free

Simple API

- Offers easy to use interfaces for storage and querying data provided
- APIs allow low-level data manipulation & selection methods
- Text-based protocols mostly used with HTTP REST with JSON
- Mostly used no standard based query language
- Web-enabled databases running as internet-facing services

Distributed

- Multiple NoSQL databases can be executed in a distributed fashion
- Offers auto-scaling and fail-over capabilities
- Often ACID concept can be sacrificed for scalability and throughput
- Mostly no synchronous replication between distributed nodes Asynchronous Multi-Master Replication, peer-to-peer, HDFS Replication
- Only providing eventual consistency
- Shared Nothing Architecture. This enables less coordination and higher distribution.

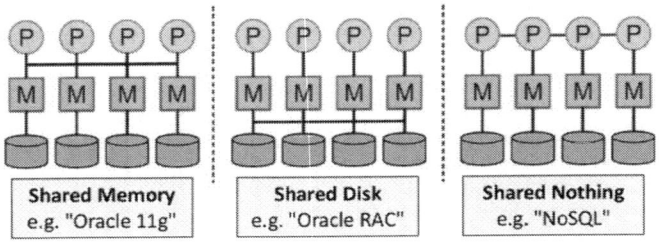

NoSQL is Shared Nothing.

Types of NoSQL Databases

  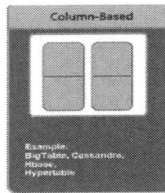 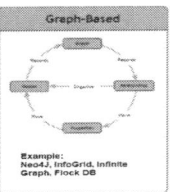

There are mainly four categories of NoSQL databases. Each of these categories has its unique attributes and limitations. No specific database is better to solve all problems. You should select a database based on your product needs.

Let see all of them:

- **Key-value Pair Based**
- **Column-oriented Graph**
- **Graphs based**
- **Document-oriented**

Key Value Pair Based
Data is stored in key/value pairs. It is designed in such a way to handle lots of data and heavy load.
Key-value pair storage databases store data as a hash table where each key is unique, and the value can be a JSON, BLOB(Binary Large Objects), string, etc.
For example, a key-value pair may contain a key like "Website" associated with a value likeneAjitVoice".

Key	Value
Name	Joe Bloggs
Age	42
Occupation	Stunt Double
Height	175cm
Weight	77kg

14

It is one of the most basic types of NoSQL databases. This kind of NoSQL database is used as a collection, dictionaries, associative arrays, etc. Key value stores help the developer to store schema-less data. They work best for shopping cart contents.

Redis, Dynamo, Riak are some examples of key-value store DataBases. They are all based on Amazon's Dynamo paper.

Column-based

Column-oriented databases work on columns and are based on BigTable paper by Google. Every column is treated separately. Values of single column databases are stored contiguously.

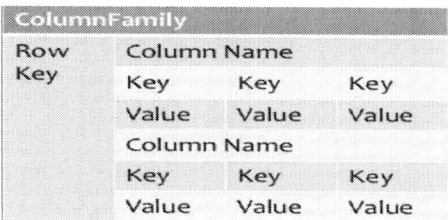

Column based NoSQL database

They deliver high performance on aggregation queries like SUM, COUNT, AVG, MIN etc. as the data is readily available in a column.

Column-based NoSQL databases are widely used to manage data warehouses, business intelligence, CRM, Library card catalogs,

HBase, Cassandra, HBase, Hypertable are examples of column based database.

Document-Oriented:

Document-Oriented NoSQL DB stores and retrieves data as a key value pair but the value part is stored as a document. The document is stored in JSON or XML formats. The value is understood by the DB and can be queried.

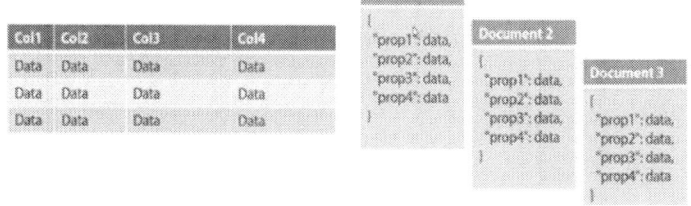

Relational Vs. Document

In this diagram on your left you can see we have rows and columns, and in the right, we have a document database which has a similar structure to JSON. Now for the relational database, you have to know what columns you have and so on. However, for a document database, you have data store like JSON object. You do not require to define which make it flexible.

The document type is mostly used for CMS systems, blogging platforms, real-time analytics & e-commerce applications. It should not use for complex transactions which require multiple operations or queries against varying aggregate structures.

Amazon SimpleDB, CouchDB, MongoDB, Riak, Lotus Notes, MongoDB, are popular Document originated DBMS systems.

Graph-Based

A graph type database stores entities as well the relations amongst those entities. The entity is stored as a node with the relationship as edges. An edge gives a relationship between nodes. Every node and edge has a unique identifier.

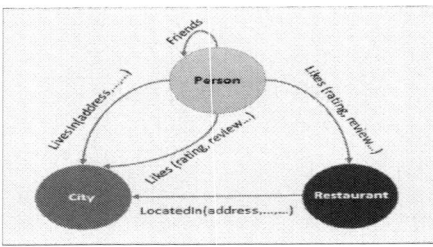

Compared to a relational database where tables are loosely connected, a Graph database is a multi-relational in nature. Traversing relationship is fast as they are already captured into the DB, and there is no need to calculate them.

Graph base database mostly used for social networks, logistics, spatial data.

Neo4J, Infinite Graph, OrientDB, FlockDB are some popular graph-based databases.

Query Mechanism tools for NoSQL

The most common data retrieval mechanism is the REST-based retrieval of a value based on its key/ID with GET resource

Document store Database offers more difficult queries as they understand the value in a key-value pair. For example, CouchDB allows defining views with MapReduce

What is the CAP Theorem?

CAP theorem is also called brewer's theorem. It states that is impossible for a distributed data store to offer more than two out of three guarantees

1. **Consistency**
2. **Availability**
3. **Partition Tolerance**

Consistency:

The data should remain consistent even after the execution of an operation. This means once data is written, any future read request should contain that data. For example, after updating the order status, all the clients should be able to see the same data.

Availability:

The database should always be available and responsive. It should not have any downtime.

Partition Tolerance:

Partition Tolerance means that the system should continue to function even if the communication among the servers is not stable. For example, the servers can be partitioned into multiple groups which may not communicate with each other. Here, if part of the database is unavailable, other parts are always unaffected.

Eventual Consistency

The term "eventual consistency" means to have copies of data on multiple machines to get high availability and scalability. Thus, changes made to any data item on one machine has to be propagated to other replicas.

Data replication may not be instantaneous as some copies will be updated immediately while others in due course of time. These copies may be mutually, but in due course of time, they become consistent. Hence, the name eventual consistency.

BASE: Basically Available, Soft state, Eventual consistency

- Basically, available means DB is available all the time as per CAP theorem
- Soft state means even without an input; the system state may change
- Eventual consistency means that the system will become consistent over time

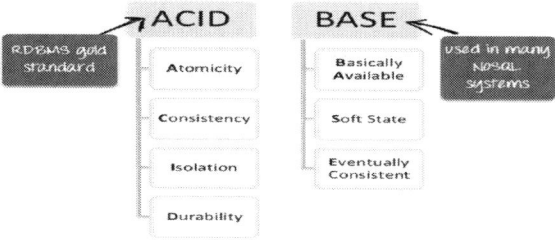

Advantages of NoSQL

- Can be used as Primary or Analytic Data Source
- Big Data Capability
- No Single Point of Failure
- Easy Replication
- No Need for Separate Caching Layer
- It provides fast performance and horizontal scalability.
- Can handle structured, semi-structured, and unstructured data with equal effect
- Object-oriented programming which is easy to use and flexible
- NoSQL databases don't need a dedicated high-performance server

- Support Key Developer Languages and Platforms
- Simple to implement than using RDBMS
- It can serve as the primary data source for online applications.
- Handles big data which manages data velocity, variety, volume, and complexity
- Excels at distributed database and multi-data center operations
- Eliminates the need for a specific caching layer to store data
- Offers a flexible schema design which can easily be altered without downtime or service disruption

Disadvantages of NoSQL

- No standardization rules
- Limited query capabilities
- RDBMS databases and tools are comparatively mature
- It does not offer any traditional database capabilities, like consistency when multiple transactions are performed simultaneously.
- When the volume of data increases it is difficult to maintain unique values as keys become difficult
- Doesn't work as well with relational data
- The learning curve is stiff for new developers
- Open source options so not so popular for enterprises.

When To Use MongoDB

By now you should have a feel for where and how MongoDB might fit into your existing system. There are enough new and competing storage technologies that it's easy to get overwhelmed by all of the choices.

For me, the most important lesson, which has nothing to do with MongoDB, is that you no longer have to rely on a single solution for dealing with your data. No doubt, a single solution has obvious advantages, and for a lot projects - possibly even most - a single solution is the sensible approach. The idea isn't that you *must* use different technologies, but rather that you *can*. Only you know whether the benefits of introducing a new solution outweigh the costs.

With that said, I'm hopeful that what you've seen so far has made you see MongoDB as a general solution. It's been mentioned a couple times that document-oriented databases share a lot in common with relational databases. Therefore, rather than tiptoeing around it, let's simply state that MongoDB should be seen as a direct alternative to relational databases. Where one might see Lucene as enhancing a relational database with full text indexing, or Redis as a persistent key-value store, MongoDB is a central repository for your data.

Notice that I didn't call MongoDB a *replacement* for relational databases, but rather an *alternative*. It's a tool that can do what a lot of other tools can do. Some of it MongoDB does better, some of it MongoDB does worse. Let's dissect things a little further.

Flexible Schema

An oft-touted benefit of document-oriented database is that they don't enforce a fixed schema. This makes them much more flexible than traditional database tables. I agree that flexible schema is a nice feature, but not for the main reason most people mention.

People talk about schema-less as though you'll suddenly start storing a crazy mishmash of data. There are domains and data sets which can really be a pain to model using relational databases, but I see those as edge cases. Schema-less is cool, but most of your data is going to be highly structured. It's true that having an occasional mismatch can be handy, especially when you introduce new features, but in reality it's nothing a nullable column probably wouldn't solve just as well.

For me, the real benefit of dynamic schema is the lack of setup and the reduced friction with OOP. This is particularly true when you're working with a static language. I've worked with MongoDB in both C# and Ruby, and the difference is striking. Ruby's dynamism and its popular ActiveRecord implementations already reduce much of the object-relational impedance mismatch. That isn't to say MongoDB isn't a good match for Ruby, it really is. Rather, I think most Ruby developers would see MongoDB as an incremental improvement, whereas C# or Java developers would see a fundamental shift in how they interact with their data.

Think about it from the perspective of a driver developer. You want to save an object? Serialize it to JSON (technically BSON, but close enough) and send it to MongoDB. There is no property mapping or type mapping. This straightfor-wardness definitely flows to you, the end developer.

Writes

One area where MongoDB can fit a specialized role is in logging. There are two aspects of MongoDB which make writes quite fast. First, you have an option to send a write command and have it return immediately without waiting for the write to be acknowledged. Secondly, you can control the write behavior with respect to data durability. These settings, in addition to specifying how many servers should get your data before being considered successful, are configurable per-write, giving you a great level of control over write performance and data durability.

In addition to these performance factors, log data is one of those data sets which can often take advantage of schema-less collections. Finally, MongoDB has something called a capped collection. So far, all of the implicitly created collec-tions we've created are just normal collections. We can create a capped collection by using the db.createCollection command and flagging it as capped:

//limit our capped collection to 1 megabyte
db.createCollection('logs', {capped: **true**, size: 1048576})

When our capped collection reaches its 1MB limit, old documents are automatically purged. A limit on the number of documents, rather than the size, can be set using max. Capped collections have some interesting properties. For example, you can update a document but it can't change in size. The insertion order is preserved, so you don't need to add an extra index to get proper time-based sorting. You can "tail" a capped collection the way you tail a file in Unix via tail -f <filename> which allows you to get new data as it arrives, without having to re-query it.

If you want to "expire" your data based on time rather than overall collection size, you can use TTL Indexes where TTL stands for "time-to-live".

Durability

Prior to version 1.8, MongoDB did not have single-server durability. That is, a server crash would likely result in lost or corrupt data. The solution had always been to run MongoDB in a multi-server setup (MongoDB supports replication). Journaling was one of the major features added in 1.8. Since version 2.0 MongoDB enables journaling by default, which allows fast recovery of the server in case of a crash or abrupt power loss.

Durability is only mentioned here because a lot has been made around MongoDB's past lack of single-server durability. This'll likely show up in Google searches for some time to come. Information you find about journaling being a missing feature is simply out of date.

Full Text Search

True full text search capability is a recent addition to MongoDB. It supports fifteen languages with stemming and stop words. With MongoDB's support for arrays and full text search you will only need to look to other solutions if you need a more powerful and full-featured full text search engine.

Transactions

MongoDB doesn't have transactions. It has two alternatives, one which is great but with limited use, and the other that is cumbersome but flexible.

The first is its many atomic update operations. These are great, so long as they actually address your problem. We already saw some of the simpler ones, like $inc and $set. There are also commands like findAndModify which can update or delete a document and return it atomically.

The second, when atomic operations aren't enough, is to fall back to a two-phase commit. A two-phase commit is to transactions what manual dereferencing is to joins. It's a storage-agnostic solution that you do in code. Two-phase commits are actually quite popular in the relational world as a way to implement transactions across multiple databases. The MongoDB website has an example illustrating the most typical example (a transfer of funds). The general idea is that you store the state of the transaction within the actual document being updated atomically and go through the init-pending-commit/rollback steps manually.

MongoDB's support for nested documents and flexible schema design makes two-phase commits slightly less painful, but it still isn't a great process, especially when you are just getting started with it.

Data Processing

Before version 2.2 MongoDB relied on MapReduce for most data processing jobs. As of 2.2 it has added a powerful feature called aggregation framework or pipeline, so you'll only need to use MapReduce in rare cases where you need complex functions for aggregations that are not yet supported in the pipeline. In the next chapter we'll look at Aggregation Pipeline and MapReduce in detail. For now you can think of them as feature-rich and different ways to group by (which is an understatement). For parallel processing of very large data, you may need to rely on something else, such as Hadoop. Thankfully, since the two systems really do complement each other, there's a MongoDB connector for Hadoop.

Of course, parallelizing data processing isn't something relational databases excel at either. There are plans for future versions of MongoDB to be better at handling very large sets of data.

Geospatial

A particularly powerful feature of MongoDB is its support for geospatial indexes. This allows you to store either geoJSON or x and y coordinates within documents and then find documents that are $near a set of coordinates or $within a box or circle. This is a feature best explained via some visual aids, so I invite you to try the 5 minute geospatial interactive tutorial, if you want to learn more.

Tools and Maturity

You probably already know the answer to this, but MongoDB is obviously younger than most relational database systems. This is absolutely something you should consider, though how much it matters depends on what you are doing and how you are doing it. Nevertheless, an honest assessment simply can't ignore the fact that MongoDB is younger and the available tooling around isn't great (although the tooling around a lot of very mature relational databases is pretty horrible too!). As an example, the lack of support for base-10 floating point numbers will obviously be a concern (though not necessarily a show-stopper) for systems dealing with money.

Section 1.1: Execution of a JavaScript file in MongoDB

./mongo localhost:27017/mydb myjsfile.js

Explanation: This operation executes the myjsfile.js script in a mongo shell that connects to the mydb database on the mongod instance accessible via the localhost interface on port 27017. localhost:27017 is not mandatory as this is the default port mongodb uses.
Also, you can run a .js file from within mongo console.
>load("myjsfile.js")

Section 1.2: Making the output of find readable in shell

We add three records to our collection test as:
db.test.insert({"key":"value1","key2":"Val2","key3":"val3"}) WriteResult({ "nInserted" : 1 })
db.test.insert({"key":"value2","key2":"Val21","key3":"val31"}) WriteResult({ "nInserted" : 1 })
db.test.insert({"key":"value3","key2":"Val22","key3":"val33"}) WriteResult({ "nInserted" : 1 })

If we see them via find, they will look very ugly.
> db.test.find()

{ "_id" : ObjectId("5790c5cecae25b3d38c3c7ae"), "key" : "value1", "key2" : "Val2 ", "key3" : "val3" }
{ "_id" : ObjectId("5790c5d9cae25b3d38c3c7af"), "key" : "value2", "key2" : "Val2 1", "key3" : "val31" }
{ "_id" : ObjectId("5790c5e9cae25b3d38c3c7b0"), "key" : "value3", "key2" : "Val2 2", "key3" : "val33" }

To work around this and make them readable, use the **pretty**() function.
> db.test.find().pretty()
{
"_id" : ObjectId("5790c5cecae25b3d38c3c7ae"), "key" : "value1","key2" : "Val2", "key3" : "val3"
}
{
"_id" : ObjectId("5790c5d9cae25b3d38c3c7af"), "key" : "value2","key2" : "Val21", "key3" : "val31"
}
{
"_id" : ObjectId("5790c5e9cae25b3d38c3c7b0"), "key" : "value3","key2" : "Val22", "key3" : "val33"
}
>

Section 1.3: Complementary Terms

SQL Terms	MongoDB Terms
Database	Database
Table	Collection
Entity / Row	Document
Column	Key / Field
Table Join	Embedded Documents
Primary Key	Primary Key (Default key _id provided by mongodb itself)

Section 1.4: Installation

To install MongoDB, follow the steps below:

Install MongoDB On Windows

To install MongoDB on Windows, first download the latest release of MongoDB from https://www.mongodb.org/downloads. Make sure you get correct version of MongoDB depending upon your Windows version. To get your Windows version, open command prompt and execute the following command.

```
C:\>wmic os get osarchitecture
OSArchitecture
64-bit
C:\>
```

32-bit versions of MongoDB only support databases smaller than 2GB and suitable only for testing and evaluation purposes.
Now extract your downloaded file to c:\ drive or any other location. Make sure the name of the extracted folder is mongodb-win32-i386-[version] or mongodb-win32-x86_64-[version]. Here [version] is the version of MongoDB download e.g 4.0.
Next, open the command prompt and run the following command.

```
C:\>move mongodb-win64-* mongodb
   1 dir(s) moved.
C:\>
```

In case you have extracted the MongoDB at different location, then go to that path by using command cd FOLDER/DIR and now run the above given process.
MongoDB requires a data folder to store its files. The default location for the MongoDB data directory is c:\data\db. So you need to create this folder using the Command Prompt. Execute the following command sequence.

```
C:\>md data
C:\md data\db
```

If you have to install the MongoDB at a different location, then you need to specify an alternate path for \data\db by setting the path dbpath in mongod.exe. For the same, issue the following commands.
In the command prompt, navigate to the bin directory present in the MongoDB installation folder. Suppose my installation folder is D:\set up\mongodb

```
C:\Users\XYZ>d:
D:\>cd "set up"
D:\set up>cd mongodb
D:\set up\mongodb>cd bin
D:\set up\mongodb\bin>mongod.exe --dbpath "d:\set up\mongodb\data"
```

This will show waiting for connections message on the console output, which indicates that the mongod.exe process is running successfully.
Now to run the MongoDB, you need to open another command prompt and issue the following command.

```
D:\set up\mongodb\bin>mongo.exe
MongoDB shell version: 4.0
connecting to: test
>db.test.save( { a: 1 } )
>db.test.find()
{ "_id" : ObjectId(5879b0f65a56a454), "a" : 1 }
>
```

This will show that MongoDB is installed and run successfully. Next time when you run MongoDB, you need to issue only commands.

```
D:\set up\mongodb\bin>mongod.exe --dbpath "d:\set up\mongodb\data"
D:\set up\mongodb\bin>mongo.exe
```

Install MongoDB on Ubuntu

Run the following command to import the MongoDB public GPG key –

```
sudo apt-key adv --keyserver hkp://keyserver.ubuntu.com:80 --recv 7F0CEB10
```

Create a /etc/apt/sources.list.d/mongodb.list file using the following command.

```
echo 'deb http://downloads-distro.mongodb.org/repo/ubuntu-upstart dist 10gen'
  | sudo tee /etc/apt/sources.list.d/mongodb.list
```

Now issue the following command to update the repository –

```
sudo apt-get update
```

Next install the MongoDB by using the following command –

```
apt-get install mongodb-10gen = 4.0
```

In the above installation, 4.0 is currently released MongoDB version. Make sure to install the latest version always. Now MongoDB is installed successfully.

Start MongoDB
sudo service mongodb start
Stop MongoDB
sudo service mongodb stop
Restart MongoDB
sudo service mongodb restart
To use MongoDB run the following command.
mongo

This will connect you to running MongoDB instance.

MongoDB Help
To get a list of commands, type db.help() in MongoDB client. This will give you a list of commands as shown in the following screenshot.

MongoDB Statistics
To get stats about MongoDB server, type the command db.stats() in MongoDB client. This will show the database name, number of collection and documents in the database. Output of the command is shown in the following screenshot.

Section 1.5: Basic commands on mongo shell

Show all available databases:
show dbs;

Select a particular database to access, e.g. mydb. This will create mydb if it does not already exist:
use mydb;

Show all collections in the database (be sure to select one first, see above):
show collections;

Show all functions that can be used with the database:
db.mydb.help();

To check your currently selected database, use the command db
> db mydb

To drop a existing database.
db.dropDatabase()
db.dropDatabase()

Section 1.6: Hello World

After installation process, the following lines should be entered in mongo shell (client terminal).
db.world.insert({ "speech" : "Hello World!" });

cur = db.world.find();x=cur.next();print(x["speech"]);
Hello World!

Explanation:
In the first line, we have inserted a { key : value } paired document in the default database test and in the collection named world.

In the second line we retrieve the data we have just inserted. The retrieved data is kept in a javascript variable named cur. Then by the next() function, we retrieved the first and only document and kept it in another js variable named x. Then printed the value of the document providing the key.

Chapter 2:
CRUD Operation

MongoDB - Create Database

The use Command
MongoDB **use DATABASE_NAME** is used to create database. The command will create a new database if it doesn't exist, otherwise it will return the existing database.
Syntax

use DATABASE_NAME

Example
If you want to use a database with name **<mydb>**, then **use DATABASE** statement would be as follows

>use mydb switched to db mydb

To check your currently selected database, use the command **db**

>db mydb

If you want to check your databases list, use the command **show dbs**.

>show dbs local   0.78125GB test   0.23012GB

Your created database (mydb) is not present in list. To display database, you need to insert at least one document into it.

>db.movie.insert({"name":"tutorials point"}) >show dbs local   0.78125GB mydb   0.23012GB test   0.23012GB

In MongoDB default database is test. If you didn't create any database, then collections will be stored in test database.

MongoDB - Drop Database
The dropDatabase() Method
MongoDB **db.dropDatabase()** command is used to drop a existing database.
Syntax

db.dropDatabase()

This will delete the selected database. If you have not selected any database, then it will delete default 'test' database.
Example
First, check the list of available databases by using the command, **show dbs**.

>show dbs local   0.78125GB mydb   0.23012GB test   0.23012GB >

If you want to delete new database **<mydb>**, then **dropDatabase()** command would be as follows –

>use mydb switched to db mydb >db.dropDatabase() >{ "dropped" : "mydb", "ok" : 1 } >

Now check list of databases.

```
>show dbs
local    0.78125GB
test     0.23012GB
>
```

MongoDB - Create Collection

The createCollection() Method

MongoDB **db.createCollection(name, options)** is used to create collection.

Syntax

```
db.createCollection(name, options)
```

In the command, **name** is name of collection to be created. **Options** is a document and is used to specify configuration of collection.

Parameter	Type	Description
Name	String	Name of the collection to be created
Options	Document	(Optional) Specify options about memory size and indexing

Options parameter is optional, so you need to specify only the name of the collection. Following is the list of options you can use −

Field	Type	Description
capped	Boolean	(Optional) If true, enables a capped collection. Capped collection is a fixed size collection that automatically overwrites its oldest entries when it reaches its maximum size. **If you specify true, you need to specify size parameter also.**
autoIndexId	Boolean	(Optional) If true, automatically create index on _id field.s Default value is false.
size	number	(Optional) Specifies a maximum size in bytes for a capped collection. **If capped is true, then you need to specify this field also.**
max	number	(Optional) Specifies the maximum number of documents allowed in the capped collection.

While inserting the document, MongoDB first checks size field of capped collection, then it checks max field.

Examples

Basic syntax of **createCollection()** method without options is as follows −

```
>use test
switched to db test
>db.createCollection("mycollection")
{ "ok" : 1 }
>
```

You can check the created collection by using the command **show collections**.

```
>show collections
mycollection
system.indexes
```

The following example shows the syntax of **createCollection()** method with few important options −

```
>db.createCollection("mycol", { capped : true, autoIndexId : true, size :
   6142800, max : 10000 } )
{ "ok" : 1 }
>
```

In MongoDB, you don't need to create collection. MongoDB creates collection automatically, when you insert some document.

```
>db.tutorialspoint.insert({"name" : "Ajitcollection"})
>show collections
mycol
mycollection
system.indexes
Ajitcollection
>
```

MongoDB - Drop Collection
The drop() Method
MongoDB's **db.collection.drop()** is used to drop a collection from the database.
Syntax
Basic syntax of **drop()** command is as follows -

```
db.COLLECTION_NAME.drop()
```

Example
First, check the available collections into your database **mydb**.

```
>use mydb
switched to db mydb
>show collections
mycol
mycollection
system.indexes
Ajitcollection
>
```

Now drop the collection with the name **mycollection**.

```
>db.mycollection.drop()
true
>
```

Again check the list of collections into database.

```
>show collections
mycol
system.indexes
Ajitcollection
>
```

drop() method will return true, if the selected collection is dropped successfully, otherwise it will return false.

Data Types
MongoDB supports many datatypes. Some of them are -
- **String** - This is the most commonly used datatype to store the data. String in MongoDB must be UTF-8 valid.
- **Integer** - This type is used to store a numerical value. Integer can be 32 bit or 64 bit depending upon your server.
- **Boolean** - This type is used to store a boolean (true/ false) value.
- **Double** - This type is used to store floating point values.
- **Min/ Max keys** - This type is used to compare a value against the lowest and highest BSON elements.
- **Arrays** - This type is used to store arrays or list or multiple values into one key.
- **Timestamp** - ctimestamp. This can be handy for recording when a document has been modified or added.
- **Object** - This datatype is used for embedded documents.
- **Null** - This type is used to store a Null value.
- **Symbol** - This datatype is used identically to a string; however, it's generally reserved for languages that use a specific symbol type.

- **Date** – This datatype is used to store the current date or time in UNIX time format. You can specify your own date time by creating object of Date and passing day, month, year into it.
- **Object ID** – This datatype is used to store the document's ID.
- **Binary data** – This datatype is used to store binary data.
- **Code** – This datatype is used to store JavaScript code into the document.
- **Regular expression** – This datatype is used to store regular expression.

Section 2.1: Create

The insert() Method
To insert data into MongoDB collection, you need to use MongoDB's insert() or save() method.
Syntax
The basic syntax of insert() command is as follows –
>db.COLLECTION_NAME.insert(document)

db.people.insert({name: 'Tom', age: 28});
Or
db.people.save({name: 'Tom', age: 28});

The difference with <u>save</u> is that if the passed document contains an _id field, if a document already exists with that _id it will be updated instead of being added as new.
Use insertOne to insert only one record:
db.people.insertOne({name: 'Tom', age: 28});

Use insertMany to insert multiple records:
db.people.insertMany([{name: 'Tom', age: 28},{name: 'John', age: 25}, {name: 'Kathy', age: 23}])

Section 2.2: Update

Update the **entire** object:
db.people.update({name: 'Tom'}, {age: 29, name: 'Tom'})

db.people.updateOne({name: 'Tom'},{age: 29, name: 'Tom'}) //Will replace only first matching document.
db.people.updateMany({name: 'Tom'},{age: 29, name: 'Tom'}) //Will replace all matching documents.

Or just update a single field of a document. In this case age: db.people.update({name: 'Tom'}, {$set: {age: 29}})

You can also update multiple documents simultaneously by adding a third parameter. This query will update all documents where the name equals Tom:
db.people.update({name: 'Tom'}, {$set: {age: 29}}, {multi: **true**})

db.people.updateOne({name: 'Tom'},{$set:{age: 30}) //Will update only first matching document.
db.people.updateMany({name: 'Tom'},{$set:{age: 30}}) //Will update all matching documents.

If a new field is coming for update, that field will be added to the document.
db.people.updateMany({name: 'Tom'},{$set:{age: 30, salary:50000}})// Document will have `salary` field as well.

If a document is needed to be replaced,
db.collection.replaceOne({name:'Tom'}, {name:'Lakmal',age:25,address:'Sri Lanka'})
can be used.

Note: Fields you use to identify the object will be saved in the updated document. Field that are not defined in the update section will be removed from the document.

Section 2.3: Delete

Deletes all documents matching the query parameter:
db.people.deleteMany({name: 'Tom'})

//All versions
db.people.remove({name: 'Tom'})

Or just one
db.people.deleteOne({name: 'Tom'})

// All versions db.people.remove({name: 'Tom'}, **true**)

MongoDB's remove() method. If you execute this command without any argument or without empty argument it will remove all documents from the collection.
db.people.remove();
or
db.people.remove({});

Section 2.4: Read
Query for all the docs in the people collection that have a name field with a value of 'Tom':
db.people.find({name: 'Tom'})
Or just the first one:
db.people.findOne({name: 'Tom'})
You can also specify which fields to return by passing a field selection parameter. The following will exclude the _id field and only include the age field:
db.people.find({name: 'Tom'}, {_id: 0, age: 1})

Note: by default, the _id field will be returned, even if you don't ask for it. If you would like not to get the _id back, you can just follow the previous example and ask for the _id to be excluded by specifying _id: 0 (or _id: **false**).If you want to find sub record like address object contains country, city, etc.
db.people.find({'address.country': 'US'})
& specify field too if required
db.people.find({'address.country': 'US'}, {'name': **true**, 'address.city': **true**})Remember that the result has a `.pretty()` method that pretty-prints resulting JSON:
db.people.find().pretty()

Section 2.5: Update of embedded documents
For the following schema:
{name: 'Tom', age: 28, marks: [50, 60, 70]}

Update Tom's marks to 55 where marks are 50 (Use the positional operator $):
db.people.update({name: "Tom", marks: 50}, {"$set": {"marks.$": 55}})

For the following schema:
{name: 'Tom', age: 28, marks: [{subject: "English", marks: 90},{subject: "Maths", marks: 100}, {subject: "Computes", marks: 20}]}

Update Tom's English marks to 85 :
db.people.update({name: "Tom", "marks.subject": "English"},{"$set":{"marks.$.marks": 85}})

Explaining above example:
By using {name: "Tom", "marks.subject": "English"} you will get the position of the object in the marks array, where subject is English. In "marks.$.marks", $ is used to update in that position of the marks array

Update Values in an Array
The positional $ operator identifies an element in an array to update without explicitly specifying the position of the element in the array.

Consider a collection students with the following documents:
{ "_id" : 1, "grades" : [80, 85, 90] } { "_id" : 2, "grades" : [88, 90, 92] } { "_id" : 3, "grades" : [85, 100, 90] }

To update 80 to 82 in the grades array in the first document, use the positional $ operator if you do not know the position of the element in the array:
db.students.update(

{ _id: 1, grades: 80 },

{ $set: { "grades.$" : 82 } }

Section 2.6: More update operators

You can use other operators besides $set when updating a document. The $push operator allows you to push a value into an array, in this case we will add a new nickname to the nicknames array.
db.people.update({name: 'Tom'}, {$push: {nicknames: 'Tommy'}})

// This adds the string 'Tommy' into the nicknames array in Tom's document.
The $pull operator is the opposite of $push, you can pull specific items from arrays.
db.people.update({name: 'Tom'}, {$pull: {nicknames: 'Tommy'}})

// This removes the string 'Tommy' from the nicknames array in Tom's document.
The $pop operator allows you to remove the first or the last value from an array. Let's say Tom's document has a property called siblings that has the value ['Marie', 'Bob', 'Kevin', 'Alex'].
db.people.update({name: 'Tom'}, {$pop: {siblings: -1}})

// This will remove the first value from the siblings array, which is 'Marie' in this case.
db.people.update({name: 'Tom'}, {$pop: {siblings: 1}})

// This will remove the last value from the siblings array, which is 'Alex' in this case.

Section 2.7: "multi" Parameter while updating multiple documents

To update multiple documents in a collection, set the multi option to true.
db.collection.update(query,
update,
{
upsert: boolean, multi: boolean, writeConcern: document
}
)

multi is optional. If set to true, updates multiple documents that meet the query criteria. If set to false, updates one document. The default value is false.

db.mycol.find() { "_id" : ObjectId(598354878df45ec5), "title":"MongoDB Overview"}
{ "_id" : ObjectId(59835487adf45ec6), "title":"NoSQL Overview"}
{ "_id" : ObjectId(59835487adf45ec7), "title":"Tutorials Point Overview"}

db.mycol.update({'title':'MongoDB Overview'}, {$set:{'title':'New MongoDB Tutorial'}},{multi:true})

Chapter 3: Querying for Data (Getting Started)

Basic querying examples

Section 3.1: Find()
retrieve all documents in a collection
db.collection.find({});

retrieve documents in a collection using a condition (similar to WHERE in MYSQL)
db.collection.find({key: value}); example
db.users.find({email:"sample@email.com"});

retrieve documents in a collection using Boolean conditions (Query Operators)
//AND db.collection.find({
$and: [

{ key: value }, { key: value }
]
})

//OR db.collection.find({
$or: [
{ key: value }, { key: value }
]
})
//NOT

db.inventory.find({ key: { $not: value } })

NOTE: *find()* will keep on searching the collection even if a document match has been found , therefore it is ine cient when used in a large collection , however by carefully modeling your data and/or using indexes you can increase the e ciency of *find()*

Section 3.2: FindOne()
db.collection.findOne({});
the querying functionality is similar to find() but this will end execution the moment it finds one document matching its condition , if used with and empty object , it will fetch the first document and return it . findOne() mongodb api documentation

Section 3.3: limit, skip, sort and count the results of the find() method
Similar to aggregation methods also by the find() method you have the possibility to limit, skip, sort and count the results. Let say we have following collection:
db.test.insertMany([

{name:"Any", age:"21", status:"busy"}, {name:"Tony", age:"25", status:"busy"}, {name:"Bobby", age:"28", status:"online"}, {name:"Sonny", age:"28", status:"away"}, {name:"Cher", age:"20", status:"online"}

])

To list the collection:
db.test.find({})
Will return:
{ "_id" : ObjectId("592516d7fbd5b591f53237b0"), "name" : "Any", "age" : "21", "status" : "busy" }
{ "_id" : ObjectId("592516d7fbd5b591f53237b1"), "name" : "Tony", "age" : "25", "status" : "busy" }
{ "_id" : ObjectId("592516d7fbd5b591f53237b2"), "name" : "Bobby", "age" : "28", "status" : "online" }
{ "_id" : ObjectId("592516d7fbd5b591f53237b3"), "name" : "Sonny", "age" : "28", "status" : "away" }
{ "_id" : ObjectId("592516d7fbd5b591f53237b4"), "name" : "Cher", "age" : "20", "status" : "online" }

To skip first 3 documents:
db.test.find({}).skip(3)
Will return:
{ "_id" : ObjectId("592516d7fbd5b591f53237b3"), "name" : "Sonny", "age" : "28", "status" : "away" }

{ "_id" : ObjectId("592516d7fbd5b591f53237b4"), "name" : "Cher", "age" : "20", "status" : "online"}

To sort descending by the field name:
db.test.find({}).sort({ "name" : -1})
Will return:
{ "_id" : ObjectId("592516d7fbd5b591f53237b1"), "name" : "Tony", "age" : "25", "status" : "busy" }
{ "_id" : ObjectId("592516d7fbd5b591f53237b3"), "name" : "Sonny", "age" : "28", "status" : "away" }
{ "_id" : ObjectId("592516d7fbd5b591f53237b4"), "name" : "Cher", "age" : "20", "status" : "online" }
{ "_id" : ObjectId("592516d7fbd5b591f53237b2"), "name" : "Bobby", "age" : "28", "status" : "online" }
{ "_id" : ObjectId("592516d7fbd5b591f53237b0"), "name" : "Any", "age" : "21", "status" : "busy" }
If you want to sort ascending just replace -1 with 1

To count the results:
db.test.find({}).count()
Will return:
5

Also combinations of this methods are allowed. For example get 2 documents from descending sorted collection skipping the first 1:
db.test.find({}).sort({ "name" : -1}).skip(1).limit(2)
Will return:
{ "_id" : ObjectId("592516d7fbd5b591f53237b3"), "name" : "Sonny", "age" : "28", "status" : "away" }
{ "_id" : ObjectId("592516d7fbd5b591f53237b4"), "name" : "Cher", "age" : "20", "status" : "online" }

Section 3.4: Query Document - Using AND, OR and IN Conditions
All documents from students collection.
> db.students.find().pretty();
{
"_id" : ObjectId("58f29a694117d1b7af126dca"), "studentNo" : 1,
"firstName" : "Prosen", "lastName" : "Ghosh", "age" : 25
}
{
"_id" : ObjectId("58f29a694117d1b7af126dcb"), "studentNo" : 2,
"firstName" : "Rajib", "lastName" : "Ghosh", "age" : 25
}

{
"_id" : ObjectId("58f29a694117d1b7af126dcc"), "studentNo" : 3,
"firstName" : "Rizve", "lastName" : "Amin", "age" : 23
}

{
"_id" : ObjectId("58f29a694117d1b7af126dcd"), "studentNo" : 4,
"firstName" : "Jabed", "lastName" : "Bangali", "age" : 25
}
{
"_id" : ObjectId("58f29a694117d1b7af126dce"), "studentNo" : 5,
"firstName" : "Gm", "lastName" : "Anik", "age" : 23
}
Similar mySql Query of the above command.
SELECT * FROM students;

db.students.find({firstName:"Prosen"});
{ "_id" : ObjectId("58f2547804951ad51ad206f5"), "studentNo" : "1", "firstName" : "Prosen", "lastName" : "Ghosh", "age" : "23" }
Similar mySql Query of the above command.
SELECT * FROM students **WHERE** firstName = "Prosen";

AND Queries
db.students.find({ "firstName": "Prosen", "age": {
"$gte": 23
}
});
{ "_id" : ObjectId("58f29a694117d1b7af126dca"), "studentNo" : 1, "firstName" : "Prosen", "lastName" : "Ghosh", "age" : 25 }

Similar mySql Query of the above command.
SELECT FROM STUDENTS WHERE firstName = "Prosen" **AND** age >= 23

Or Queries
db.students.find({ "$or": [{
"firstName": "Prosen"

32

}, {
"age": { "$gte": 23
}
}]
});

{ "_id" : ObjectId("58f29a694117d1b7af126dca"), "studentNo" : 1, "firstName" : "Prosen", "lastName" : "Ghosh", "age" : 25 }
{ "_id" : ObjectId("58f29a694117d1b7af126dcb"), "studentNo" : 2, "firstName" : "Rajib", "lastName" : "Ghosh", "age" : 25 }
{ "_id" : ObjectId("58f29a694117d1b7af126dcc"), "studentNo" : 3, "firstName" : "Rizve", "lastName" : "Amin", "age" : 23 }
{ "_id" : ObjectId("58f29a694117d1b7af126dcd"), "studentNo" : 4, "firstName" : "Jabed", "lastName" : "Bangali", "age" : 25 }
{ "_id" : ObjectId("58f29a694117d1b7af126dce"), "studentNo" : 5, "firstName" : "Gm", "lastName" : "Anik", "age" : 23 }

Similar mySql Query of the above command.
SELECT FROM STUDENTS WHERE firstName = "Prosen" **OR** age >= 23

And OR Queries
db.students.find({
firstName : "Prosen", $or : [
{age : 23}, {age : 25}
]
});
{ "_id" : ObjectId("58f29a694117d1b7af126dca"), "studentNo" : 1, "firstName" : "Prosen", "lastName" : "Ghosh", "age" : 25 }
Similar mySql Query of the above command.
SELECT * FROM students **WHERE** firstName = "Prosen" **AND** age = 23 **OR** age = 25;

IN Queries This queries can improve multiple use of OR Queries
db.students.find(lastName:{$in:["Ghosh", "Amin"]})
{ "_id" : ObjectId("58f29a694117d1b7af126dca"), "studentNo" : 1, "firstName" : "Prosen", "lastName" : "Ghosh", "age" : 25 }
{ "_id" : ObjectId("58f29a694117d1b7af126dcb"), "studentNo" : 2, "firstName" : "Rajib", "lastName" : "Ghosh", "age" : 25 }
{ "_id" : ObjectId("58f29a694117d1b7af126dcc"), "studentNo" : 3, "firstName" : "Rizve", "lastName" : "Amin", "age" : 23 }

Similar mySql query to above command
SELECT * FROM students **WHERE** lastName **IN** ('Ghosh', 'Amin')

Section 3.5: find() method with Projection
The basic syntax of find() method with projection is as follows
> db.COLLECTION_NAME.find({},{KEY:1});
If you want to show all documents without the age field then the command is as follows
db.people.find({},{age : 0});
If you want to show all documents the age field then the command is as follows

Section 3.6: Find() method with Projection
In MongoDB, projection means selecting only the necessary data rather than selecting whole of the data of a document.
The basic syntax of find() method with projection is as follows
> db.COLLECTION_NAME.find({},{KEY:1});
If you want to to show all document without the age field then the command is as follows
> db.people.find({},{age:0});
// If you want to show only the age field then the command is as follows
> db.people.find({},{age:1});

Note: _id field is always displayed while executing find() method, if you don't want this field, then you need to set it as 0.
> db.people.find({},{name:1,_id:0});
Note: 1 is used to show the field while 0 is used to hide the fields.

Section 3.6: Update Operators
parameters	Meaning
fieldName	Field will be updated :{*name*: 'Tom'}
targetVaule	Value will be assigned to the field :{name: *Tom*}

Section 3.7: $set operator to update specified field(s) in document(s)

I.Overview
A significant difference between MongoDB & RDBMS is MongoDB has many kinds of operators. One of them is update operator, which is used in update statements.

II. What happen if we don't use update operators?
Suppose we have a **student** collection to store student information(Table view):

age	name	sex
20	Tom	M
25	Billy	M
18	Mary	F
40	Ken	M

One day you get a job that need to change Tom's gender from "M" to "F". That's easy, right? So you write below statement very quickly based on your RDBMS experience:
db.student.update(
{name: 'Tom'}, // *query criteria* {sex: 'F'} // *update action*
);
Let's see what is the result:

age	name	sex
		F
25	Billy	M
18	Mary	F
40	Ken	M

We lost Tom's age & name! From this example, we can know that **the whole document will be overrided** if without any update operator in update statement. This is the default behavior of MongoDB.

III. $set operator
If we want to change only the 'sex' field in Tom's document, we can use $set to specify which field(s) we want to update:
db.student.update(
{name: 'Tom'}, // *query criteria*
{$set: {sex: 'F'}} // *update action*
);
The value of $set is an object, its fields stands for those fields you want to update in the documents, and the values of these fields are the target values.

So, the result is correct now:
Also, if you want to change both 'sex' and 'age' at the same time, you can append them to $set :
db.student.update(
{name: 'Tom'}, // *query criteria*

{$set: {sex: 'F', age: 40}} // *update action*
);

Chapter 4:
Upserts and Inserts

Section 4.1: Insert a document

_id is a 12 bytes hexadecimal number which assures the uniqueness of every document. You can provide _id while inserting the document. **If you didn't provide then MongoDB provide a unique id for every document.** These 12 bytes first 4 bytes for the current timestamp, next 3 bytes for machine id, next 2 bytes for process id of mongodb server and remaining 3 bytes are simple incremental value.

```
db.mycol.insert({
_id: ObjectId(7df78ad8902c), title: 'MongoDB Overview',
description: 'MongoDB is no sql database', by: 'tutorials point',
url: 'http://www.tutorialspoint.com', tags: ['mongodb', 'database', 'NoSQL'], likes: 100
})
```

Here *mycol* is a collection name, if the collection doesn't exist in the database, then MongoDB will create this collection and then insert document into it. In the inserted document if we don't specify the *_id* parameter, then MongoDB assigns an unique ObjectId for this document.

Section 4.2: Data Modeling

Let's shift gears and have a more abstract conversation about MongoDB. Explaining a few new terms and some new syntax is a trivial task. Having a conversation about modeling with a new paradigm isn't as easy. The truth is that most of us are still finding out what works and what doesn't when it comes to modeling with these new technologies. It's a conversation we can start having, but ultimately you'll have to practice and learn on real code.

Out of all NoSQL databases, document-oriented databases are probably the most similar to relational databases - at least when it comes to modeling. However, the differences that exist are important.

No Joins

The first and most fundamental difference that you'll need to get comfortable with is MongoDB's lack of joins. I don't know the specific reason why some type of join syntax isn't supported in MongoDB, but I do know that joins are generally seen as non-scalable. That is, once you start to split your data horizontally, you end up performing your joins on the client (the application server) anyway. Regardless of the reasons, the fact remains that data *is* relational, and MongoDB doesn't support joins.

Without knowing anything else, to live in a join-less world, we have to do joins ourselves within our application's code. Essentially we need to issue a second query to find the relevant data in a second collection. Setting our data up isn't any different than declaring a foreign key in a relational database. Let's give a little less focus to our beautiful unicorns and a bit more time to our employees. The first thing we'll do is create an employee (I'm providing an explicit _id so that we can build coherent examples)

```
db.employees.insert({_id: ObjectId(
    "4d85c7039ab0fd70a117d730"),
    name: 'Leto'})
```

Now let's add a couple employees and set their manager as Leto:
```
db.employees.insert({_id:
    ObjectId( "4d85c7039ab0fd
    70a117d731"),    name:
    'Duncan',
    manager:
    ObjectId( "4d85c7039ab0f
    d70a117d730")});
```

```
db.employees.insert({_id:
    ObjectId( "4d85c7039ab0fd
    70a117d732"),    name:
    'Moneo',
    manager:
    ObjectId( "4d85c7039ab0f
    d70a117d730")});
```

(It's worth repeating that the _id can be any unique value. Since you'd likely use an ObjectId in real life, we'll use them here as well.)

Of course, to find all of Leto's employees, one simply executes:

```
db.employees.find({manager: ObjectId(
    "4d85c7039ab0fd70a117d730")})
```

There's nothing magical here. In the worst cases, most of the time, the lack of join will merely require an extra query (likely indexed).

Arrays and Embedded Documents

Just because MongoDB doesn't have joins doesn't mean it doesn't have a few tricks up its sleeve. Remember when we saw that MongoDB supports arrays as first class objects of a document? It turns out that this is incredibly handy when dealing with many-to-one or many-to-many relationships. As a simple example, if an employee could have two managers, we could simply store these in an array:

```
db.employees.insert({_id: ObjectId(
    "4d85c7039ab0fd70a117d733"),
    name: 'Siona',
    manager: [ObjectId(
    "4d85c7039ab0fd70a117d730"),
    ObjectId(
    "4d85c7039ab0fd70a117d732")] })
```

Of particular interest is that, for some documents, manager can be a scalar value, while for others it can be an array.

Our original find query will work for both:

```
db.employees.find({manager: ObjectId(
    "4d85c7039ab0fd70a117d730")})
```

You'll quickly find that arrays of values are much more convenient to deal with than many-to-many join-tables.

Besides arrays, MongoDB also supports embedded documents. Go ahead and try inserting a document with a nested document, such as:

```
db.employees.insert({_id:
    ObjectId( "4d85c7039ab0fd
    70a117d734"),      name:
    'Ghanima',
    family:      {mother:
        'Chani',    father:
        'Paul',    brother:
        ObjectId(
    "4d85c7039ab0fd70a117d730")}})
```

In case you are wondering, embedded documents can be queried using a dot-notation:
```
db.employees.find({
    'family.mother': 'Chani'})
```

We'll briefly talk about where embedded documents fit and how you should use them.

Combining the two concepts, we can even embed arrays of documents:

```
db.employees.insert({_id:
    ObjectId( "4d85c7039ab0fd
    70a117d735"),      name:
    'Chani',
    family: [ {relation:'mother',name: 'Chani'},
        {relation:'father',name: 'Paul'},
{relation:'brother', name: 'Duncan'}]})
```

Denormalization

Yet another alternative to using joins is to denormalize your data. Historically, denormalization was reserved for performance-sensitive code, or when data should be snapshotted (like in an audit log). However, with the ever-growing popularity of NoSQL, many of which don't have joins, denormalization as part of normal modeling is becoming increasingly common. This doesn't mean you should duplicate every piece of information in every document. However, rather than letting fear of duplicate data drive your design decisions, consider modeling your data based on what information belongs to what document.

For example, say you are writing a forum application. The traditional way to associate a specific user with a post is via a userid column within posts. With such a model, you can't display posts without retrieving (joining to) users. A possible alternative is simply to store the name as well as the userid with each post. You could even do so with an embedded document, like user: {id: ObjectId('Something'), name: 'Leto'}. Yes, if you let users change their name, you may have to update each document (which is one multi-update).

Adjusting to this kind of approach won't come easy to some. In a lot of cases it won't even make sense to do this. Don't be afraid to experiment with this approach though. It's not only suitable in some circumstances, but it can also be the best way to do it.

Which Should You Choose?

Arrays of ids can be a useful strategy when dealing with one-to-many or many-to-many scenarios. But more commonly, new developers are left deciding between using embedded documents versus doing "manual" referencing.

First, you should know that an individual document is currently limited to 16 megabytes in size. Knowing that documents have a size limit, though quite generous, gives you some idea of how they are intended to be used. At this point, it seems like most developers lean heavily on manual references for most of their relationships. Embedded documents are frequently leveraged, but mostly for smaller pieces of data which we want to always pull with the parent document. A real world example may be to store an addresses documents with each user, something like:

```
db.users.insert({name:
    'leto',           email:
    'leto@dune.gov',
    addresses: [{street: "229 W. 43rd St",
             city:             "New           York",
             state:"NY",zip:"10036"}, {street: "555
             University",
             city: "Palo Alto", state:"CA",zip:"94107"}]})
```

This doesn't mean you should underestimate the power of embedded documents or write them off as something of minor utility. Having your data model map directly to your objects makes things a lot simpler and often removes the need to join. This is especially true when you consider that MongoDB lets you query and index fields of an embedded documents and arrays.

Few or Many Collections

Given that collections don't enforce any schema, it's entirely possible to build a system using a single collection with a mishmash of documents but it would be a very bad idea. Most MongoDB systems are laid out somewhat similarly to what you'd find in a relational system, though with fewer collections. In other words, if it would be a table in a relational database, there's a chance it'll be a collection in MongoDB (many-to-many join tables being an important exception as well as tables that exist only to enable one to many relationships with simple entities).

The conversation gets even more interesting when you consider embedded documents. The example that frequently comes up is a blog. Should you have a posts collection and a comments collection, or should each post have an array of comments embedded within it? Setting aside the 16MB document size limit for the time being (all of *Hamlet* is less than 200KB, so just how popular is your blog?), most developers should prefer to separate things out. It's simply cleaner, gives you better performance and more explicit. MongoDB's flexible schema allows you to combine the two approaches by keeping comments in their own collection but embedding a few comments (maybe the first few) in the blog post to be able to display them with the post. This follows the principle of keeping together data that you want to get back in one query.

There's no hard rule (well, aside from 16MB). Play with different approaches and you'll get a sense of what does and does not feel right.

A Schema for MongoDb ?

In relational databases the schema must be created before data can be stored in the database (this is done using CREATE TABLE...). In MongoDb no schema is required. We simply push the data in some collections. Nobody will tell us what to save inside. It is possible to save the companies and employees in the same collection. Most of the programmers won't do this because is hard to read this later.

DbSchema does a 'schema discovery' by scanning the database data. The schema is presented in the structure tree and diagrammed layouts. Bellow two entities were created for the 'persons' collection, one for the main document and one for the sub-document.

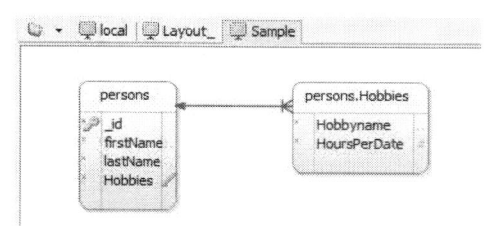

It is possible to create multiple layouts with the same or different tables. The layouts will be saved to DbSchema project file.

DbSchema use its own image of the schema, so when the database is modified you should 'refresh the schema from the database'. Using an internal image is possible to compare two different databases, open the project file without being connected to the database, etc.

Section 4.3: Join

In MongoDb you can refer one document from another document via ObjectIds. As example consider a collection 'airports' with name, location, etc., and a collection 'flights'. The flights collection may refer the 'airport' collection and not repeat each time the entire data which is stored for the airport.

Collections have assigned automatically an **_id** field (done automatically by Mongo DB when you store some data). This value can be used in the referencing collection to point to the referred collection.

Copy the example bellow in DbSchema SQL Editor. Select with the mouse one block of text (like one for statement with all following lines) and execute them one by one by pressing the 'run single query' button.

```
local.master.drop()
local.slave.drop()
for ( i = 0; i < 100; i++){
    local.master.insertOne({name: 'Master_' + i, position: i })
}

local.master.find()
for ( i = 0; i < 100; i++){
    rnd = Math.floor( Math.random() * 100 )
    masterId  =  local.master.find({position  :{  $eq  :  rnd  }}).first()._id
    local.slave.insertOne({ name: "Slave_"+i, ref : masterId })
}

local.slave.find()
```

This code is creating a collection 'master' with name and position. The next collection slave has a field ref as the **_id** of one of the master documents. You can copy-paste this in DbSchema and execute it. Refresh the schema as in the chapters before to get the collection into the diagram.

The line between collecitons is a virutal relation, meaning the 'ref' field is poiting to the 'master' collection. The virtual foreign keys are saved in the DbSchema project file.

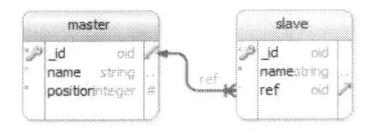

Virtual foreign key will help then in the Relational Data Browse to explore the data from two collections keeping track of the matching between them:
Press this arrow to descend into the collection 'slave'

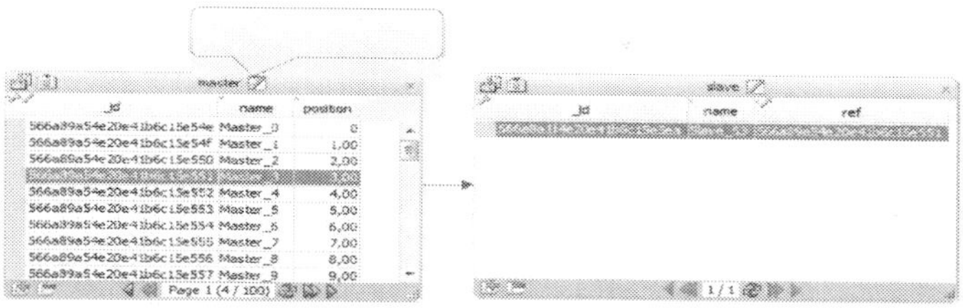

Now let's create a virtual relation. For this drag and drop the ref column over the _id column with the mouse by keeping the mouse button.

This will open the foreign key dialog.

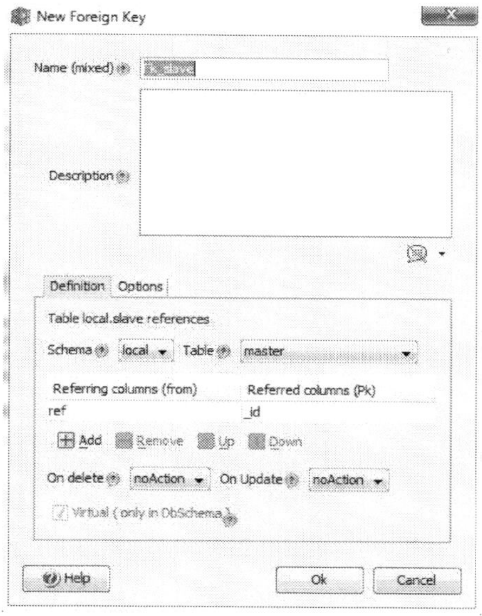

On the bottom is a checkbox 'Virtual' which is checked and disabled. All foreign keys created in

DbSchema for Mongo DB are by default virtual. The virtual relation will be painted with a distinct color.

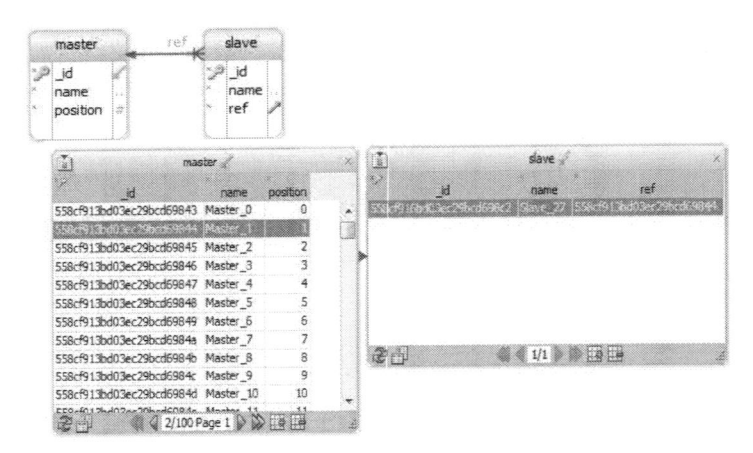

Now you can browse the data from master or slave and cascade into the other collection. The browse will show only the records corresponding to the selected record in the first browse frame.

The virtual relations are created only in DbSchema and not in the database. Save the DbSchema project to file and the virtual relations will be saved as well. Next time when you open the application the diagrams and the virtual foreign keys are available.

Chapter 5: Aggregation

Parameter	Details
pipeline	array(A sequence of data aggregation operations or stages) **options** document(optional, available only if pipeline present as an array)

Aggregations operations process data records and return computed results. Aggregation operations group values from multiple documents together, and can perform a variety of operations on the grouped data to return a single result. MongoDB provides three ways to perform aggregation: the aggregation pipeline, the map-reduce function, and single purpose aggregation methods.

From Mongo manual https://docs.mongodb.com/manual/aggregation/

Section 5.1: Count
How do you get the number of Debit and Credit transactions? One way to do it is by using count() function as below.

```
> db.transactions.count({cr_dr : "D"});
or
> db.transactions.find({cr_dr : "D"}).length();
```

But what if you do not know the possible values of cr_dr upfront. Here Aggregation framework comes to play. See the below Aggregate query.
```
> db.transactions.aggregate(
[
{
$group : {
_id : '$cr_dr', // group by type of transaction
// Add 1 for each document to the count for this type of transaction count : {$sum : 1}
}
}
]
);
```

And the result is
```
{
"_id" : "C", "count" : 3
}
{
"_id" : "D", "count" : 5
}
```

Section 5.2: Sum
How to get the summation of amount? See the below aggregate query.
```
> db.transactions.aggregate(
[
{
$group : {
_id : '$cr_dr',
count : {$sum : 1},   //counts the number
totalAmount : {$sum : '$amount'}   //sums the amount
}
}
]
);
```

And the result is
```
{
"_id" : "C", "count" : 3.0, "totalAmount" : 120.0
}
```

```
{
"_id" : "D", "count" : 5.0, "totalAmount" : 410.0
}
```

Another version that sums amount and fee.
```
> db.transactions.aggregate(
[
{
$group : {
_id : '$cr_dr', count : {$sum : 1}, totalAmount : {$sum : { $sum : ['$amount', '$fee']}}
}
}
]
);
```

And the result is
```
{
"_id" : "C", "count" : 3.0, "totalAmount" : 128.0
}
{
"_id" : "D", "count" : 5.0, "totalAmount" : 422.0
}
```

Section 5.3: Average

How to get the average amount of debit and credit transactions?
```
> db.transactions.aggregate(
[
{
$group :
{
_id : '$cr_dr',  // group by type of transaction (debit or credit)

    count : {$sum : 1},      // number of transaction for each type
    totalAmount : {$sum : { $sum : ['$amount', '$fee']}},       // sum
    averageAmount : {$avg : { $sum : ['$amount', '$fee']}}      // average
}
}
]
)
```

The result is
```
{
"_id" : "C", // Amounts for credit transactions
"count" : 3.0, "totalAmount" : 128.0, "averageAmount" : 40.0
}
{
"_id" : "D", // Amounts for debit transactions
"count" : 5.0, "totalAmount" : 422.0, "averageAmount" : 82.0
}
```

Section 5.4: Operations with arrays

When you want to work with the data entries in arrays you first need to <u>unwind</u> the array. The unwind operation creates a document for each entry in the array. When you have lot's of documents with large arrays you will see an explosion in number of documents.
```
{ "_id" : 1, "item" : "myItem1", sizes: [ "S", "M", "L"] }
{ "_id" : 2, "item" : "myItem2", sizes: [ "XS", "M", "XL"] }
db.inventory.aggregate( [ { $unwind : "$sizes" }] )
```
An important notice is that when a document doesn't contain the array it will be lost. From mongo 3.2 and up there are is an unwind option "preserveNullAndEmptyArrays" added. This option makes sure the document is preserved when the array is missing.
```
{ "_id" : 1, "item" : "myItem1", sizes: [ "S", "M", "L"] }
{ "_id" : 2, "item" : "myItem2", sizes: [ "XS", "M", "XL"] } { "_id" : 3, "item" : "myItem3" }
db.inventory.aggregate( [ { $unwind : { path: "$sizes", includeArrayIndex: "arrayIndex" } }] )
```

Section 5.5: Aggregate query examples useful for work and learning

Aggregation is used to perform complex data search operations in the mongo query which can't be done in normal "find" query.

Create some dummy data:
db.employees.insert({"name":"Adma","dept":"Admin","languages":["german","french","english","hindi"] ,"age":30, "totalExp":10});
db.employees.insert({"name":"Anna","dept":"Admin","languages":["english","hindi"],"age":35, "totalExp":11});   db.employees.insert({"name":"Bob","dept":"Facilities","languages":["english","hindi"],"age":36, "totalExp":14});
db.employees.insert({"name":"Cathy","dept":"Facilities","languages":["hindi"],"age":31, "totalExp":4});
db.employees.insert({"name":"Mike","dept":"HR","languages":["english", "hindi", "spanish"],"age":26, "totalExp":3});
db.employees.insert({"name":"Jenny","dept":"HR","languages":["english", "hindi", "spanish"],"age":25, "totalExp":3});

Examples by topic:
1. Match: Used to match documents (like SQL where clause)
db.employees.aggregate([{$match:{dept:"Admin"}}]); Output:
{ "_id" : ObjectId("54982fac2e9b4b54ec384a0d"), "name" : "Adma", "dept" : "Admin", "languages" : ["german", "french", "english", "hindi"], "age" : 30, "totalExp" : 10 }
{ "_id" : ObjectId("54982fc92e9b4b54ec384a0e"), "name" : "Anna", "dept" : "Admin", "languages" : ["english", "hindi"], "age" : 35, "totalExp" : 11 }

Project: Used to populate specific field's value(s)
project stage will include _id field automatically unless you specify to disable.
db.employees.aggregate([{$match:{dept:"Admin"}}, {$project:{"name":1, "dept":1}}]); Output:
{ "_id" : ObjectId("54982fac2e9b4b54ec384a0d"), "name" : "Adma", "dept" : "Admin" } { "_id" : ObjectId("54982fc92e9b4b54ec384a0e"), "name" : "Anna", "dept" : "Admin" }
db.employees.aggregate({$project: {_id:0, 'name': 1}}) Output:
{ "name" : "Adma" } { "name" : "Anna" } { "name" : "Bob" }
{ "name" : "Cathy" } { "name" : "Mike" } { "name" : "Jenny" }

Group: $group is used to group documents by specific field, here documents are grouped by "dept" field's value. Another useful feature is that you can group by null, it means all documents will be aggregated into one.
db.employees.aggregate([{$group:{"_id":"$dept"}}]);
{ "_id" : "HR" }
{ "_id" : "Facilities" } { "_id" : "Admin" }
db.employees.aggregate([{$group:{"_id":**null**, "totalAge":{$sum:"$age"}}}]);

Output:
{ "_id" : **null**, "noOfEmployee" : 183 }

Sum: $sum is used to count or sum the values inside a group.
db.employees.aggregate([{$group:{"_id":"$dept", "noOfDept":{$sum:1}}}]);
Output:
{ "_id" : "HR", "noOfDept" : 2 }
{ "_id" : "Facilities", "noOfDept" : 2 } { "_id" : "Admin", "noOfDept" : 2 }

Average: Calculates average of specific field's value per group.
db.employees.aggregate([{$group:{"_id":"$dept", "noOfEmployee":{$sum:1}, "avgExp":{$avg:"$totalExp"}}}]);
Output:
{ "_id" : "HR", "noOfEmployee" : 2, "totalExp" : 3 }
{ "_id" : "Facilities", "noOfEmployee" : 2, "totalExp" : 9 } { "_id" : "Admin", "noOfEmployee" : 2, "totalExp" : 10.5 }

Minimum: Finds minimum value of a field in each group.
db.employees.aggregate([{$group:{"_id":"$dept", "noOfEmployee":{$sum:1}, "minExp":{$min:"$totalExp"}}}]);
Output:
{ "_id" : "HR", "noOfEmployee" : 2, "totalExp" : 3 }
{ "_id" : "Facilities", "noOfEmployee" : 2, "totalExp" : 4 } { "_id" : "Admin", "noOfEmployee" : 2, "totalExp" : 10 }

Maximum: Finds maximum value of a field in each group.
db.employees.aggregate([{$group:{"_id":"$dept", "noOfEmployee":{$sum:1}, "maxExp":{$max:"$totalExp"}}}]);
Output:
{ "_id" : "HR", "noOfEmployee" : 2, "totalExp" : 3 }
{ "_id" : "Facilities", "noOfEmployee" : 2, "totalExp" : 14 } { "_id" : "Admin", "noOfEmployee" : 2, "totalExp" : 11 }

Getting specific field's value from first and last document of each group: Works well when doucument result is sorted.
db.employees.aggregate([{$group:{"_id":"$age", "lasts":{$last:"$name"}, "firsts":{$first:"$name"}}}]);
Output:
{ "_id" : 25, "lasts" : "Jenny", "firsts" : "Jenny" } { "_id" : 26, "lasts" : "Mike", "firsts" : "Mike" } { "_id" : 35, "lasts" : "Cathy", "firsts" : "Anna" } { "_id" : 30, "lasts" : "Adma", "firsts" : "Adma" }

Minumum with maximum:
db.employees.aggregate([{$group:{"_id":"$dept", "noOfEmployee":{$sum:1}, "maxExp":{$max:"$totalExp"}, "minExp":{$min:"$totalExp"}}}]);
Output:
{ "_id" : "HR", "noOfEmployee" : 2, "maxExp" : 3, "minExp" : 3 }
{ "_id" : "Facilities", "noOfEmployee" : 2, "maxExp" : 14, "minExp" : 4 } { "_id" : "Admin", "noOfEmployee" : 2, "maxExp" : 11, "minExp" : 10 }

Push and addToSet: Push adds a field's value form each document in group to an array used to project data in array format, addToSet is simlar to push but it omits duplicate values.
db.employees.aggregate([{$group:{"_id":"dept", "arrPush":{$push:"$age"}, "arrSet": {$addToSet:"$age"}}}]);
Output:
{ "_id" : "dept", "arrPush" : [30, 35, 35, 35, 26, 25], "arrSet" : [25, 26, 35, 30] }

Unwind: Used to create multiple in-memory documents for each value in the specified array type field, then we can do further aggregation based on those values.
db.employees.aggregate([{$match:{"name":"Adma"}}, {$unwind:"$languages"}]); Output:
{ "_id" : ObjectId("54982fac2e9b4b54ec384a0d"), "name" : "Adma", "dept" : "HR", "languages" : "german", "age" : 30, "totalExp" : 10 }
{ "_id" : ObjectId("54982fac2e9b4b54ec384a0d"), "name" : "Adma", "dept" : "HR", "languages" : "french", "age" : 30, "totalExp" : 10 }
{ "_id" : ObjectId("54982fac2e9b4b54ec384a0d"), "name" : "Adma", "dept" : "HR", "languages" : "english", "age" : 30, "totalExp" : 10 }
{ "_id" : ObjectId("54982fac2e9b4b54ec384a0d"), "name" : "Adma", "dept" : "HR", "languages" : "hindi", "age" : 30, "totalExp" : 10 }

Sorting:
db.employees.aggregate([{$match:{dept:"Admin"}}, {$project:{"name":1, "dept":1}}, {$sort: {name: 1}}]);
Output:
{ "_id" : ObjectId("57ff3e553dedf0228d4862ac"), "name" : "Adma", "dept" : "Admin" } { "_id" : ObjectId("57ff3e5e3dedf0228d4862ad"), "name" : "Anna", "dept" : "Admin" }
db.employees.aggregate([{$match:{dept:"Admin"}}, {$project:{"name":1, "dept":1}}, {$sort: {name: -1}}]);

Output:
{ "_id" : ObjectId("57ff3e5e3dedf0228d4862ad"), "name" : "Anna", "dept" : "Admin" } { "_id" : ObjectId("57ff3e553dedf0228d4862ac"), "name" : "Adma", "dept" : "Admin" }

Skip:
db.employees.aggregate([{$match:{dept:"Admin"}}, {$project:{"name":1, "dept":1}}, {$sort: {name: -1}}, {$skip:1}]);
Output:
{ "_id" : ObjectId("57ff3e553dedf0228d4862ac"), "name" : "Adma", "dept" : "Admin" }

Limit:
db.employees.aggregate([{$match:{dept:"Admin"}}, {$project:{"name":1, "dept":1}}, {$sort: {name: -1}}, {$limit:1}]);
Output:
{ "_id" : ObjectId("57ff3e5e3dedf0228d4862ad"), "name" : "Anna", "dept" : "Admin" }

Comparison operator in projection:
db.employees.aggregate([{$match:{dept:"Admin"}}, {$project:{"name":1, "dept":1, age: {$gt: ["$age", 30]}}}]);
Output:
{ "_id" : ObjectId("57ff3e553dedf0228d4862ac"), "name" : "Adma", "dept" : "Admin", "age" : **false** } { "_id" : ObjectId("57ff3e5e3dedf0228d4862ad"), "name" : "Anna", "dept" : "Admin", "age" : **true** }

Comparison operator in match:
db.employees.aggregate([{$match:{dept:"Admin", age: {$gt:30}}}, {$project:{"name":1, "dept":1}}]);
Output:
{ "_id" : ObjectId("57ff3e5e3dedf0228d4862ad"), "name" : "Anna", "dept" : "Admin" }
List of comparison operators: $cmp, $eq, $gt, $gte, $lt, $lte, and $ne

Boolean aggregation opertor in projection:
db.employees.aggregate([{$match:{dept:"Admin"}}, {$project:{"name":1, "dept":1, age: { $and: [{ $gt: ["$age", 30] }, { $lt: ["$age", 36] }] }}}]);
Output:

{ "_id" : ObjectId("57ff3e553dedf0228d4862ac"), "name" : "Adma", "dept" : "Admin", "age" : **false** } { "_id" : ObjectId("57ff3e5e3dedf0228d4862ad"), "name" : "Anna", "dept" : "Admin", "age" : **true** }

Boolean aggregation opertor in match:
db.employees.aggregate([{$match:{dept:"Admin", $and: [{age: { $gt: 30 }}, {age: {$lt: 36 }}] }}, {$project:{"name":1, "dept":1, age: { $and: [{ $gt: ["$age", 30] }, { $lt: ["$age", 36] }] }}}]);

Output:

{ "_id" : ObjectId("57ff3e5e3dedf0228d4862ad"), "name" : "Anna", "dept" : "Admin", "age" : **true** }
List of boolean aggregation opertors: $and, $or, and $not.
Complete refrence: https://docs.mongodb.com/v3.2/reference/operator/aggregation/

Section 5.6: Match
How to write a query to get all departments where average age of employees making less than or $70000 is greather than or equal to 35?
In order to that we need to write a query to match employees that have a salary that is less than or equal to $70000. Then add the aggregate stage to group the employees by the department. Then add an accumulator with a field named e.g. average_age to find the average age per department using the $avg accumulator and below the existing $match and $group aggregates add another $match aggregate so that we're only retrieving results with an average_age that is greather than or equal to 35.

db.employees.aggregate([
{"$match": {"salary": {"$lte": 70000}}},
{"$group": {"_id": "$dept",
"average_age": {"$avg": "$age"}
}
},

{"$match": {"average_age": {"$gte": 35}}}
])

The result is:
{
"_id": "IT", "average_age": 31
}
{
"_id": "Customer Service",
"average_age": 34.5
}
{
"_id": "Finance", "average_age": 32.5
}

Section 5.7: Get sample data
To get random data from certain collection refer to $sample aggregation.
db.emplyees.aggregate({ $sample: { size:1 } })
where size stands for number of items to select.

Section 5.8: Remove docs that have a duplicate field in a collection (dedupe)

Note that the allowDiskUse: true option is optional but will help mitigate out of memory issues as this aggregation can be a memory intensive operation if your collection size is large - so i recommend to always use it.
var duplicates = [];
db.transactions.aggregate([

{ $group: {
_id: { cr_dr: "$cr_dr"},
dups: { "$addToSet": "$_id" },
count: { "$sum": 1 }
}
},

{ $match: {
count: { "$gt": 1 }
}}
],allowDiskUse: **true**}
)

.result

forEach(**function**(doc) { doc.dups.shift(); doc.dups.forEach(**function**(dupId)
{
duplicates.push(dupId);

```
    }
  )
})
```

printjson(duplicates);
Remove all duplicates in one go

```
db.transactions.remove({_id:{$in:duplicates}})
```

Section 5.9: Left Outer Join with aggregation ($Lookup)

```
let col_1 = db.collection('col_1'); let col_2 = db.collection('col_2'); col_1 .aggregate([
{ $match: { "_id": 1 } },
{
$lookup: {
from: "col_2", localField: "id",
foreignField: "id", as: "new_document"
}
}
],function (err, result){ res.send(result);
});
```

This feature was newly released in the mongodb **version 3.2** , which gives the user a stage to join one collection with the matching attributes from another collection

Section 5.10: Server Aggregation

Andrew Mao's solution. <u>Average Aggregation Queries in Meteor</u>
```
Meteor.publish("someAggregation", function (args) { var sub = this;
// This works for Meteor 0.6.5

var db = MongoInternals.defaultRemoteCollectionDriver().mongo.db;
// Your arguments to Mongo's aggregation. Make these however you want. var pipeline = [
{ $match: doSomethingWith(args) }, { $group: {
_id: whatWeAreGroupingWith(args), count: { $sum: 1 }
}}
];

db.collection("server_collection_name").aggregate( pipeline,
// Need to wrap the callback so it gets called in a Fiber.

Meteor.bindEnvironment( function(err, result) {
// Add each of the results to the subscription.

_.each(result, function(e) {

// Generate a random disposable id for aggregated documents sub.added("client_collection_name", Random.id(), {
key: e._id.somethingOfInterest, count: e.count
});
}); sub.ready();
}, function(error) {
Meteor._debug( "Error doing aggregation: " + error);
}
)
);
});
```

Section 5.11: Aggregation in a Server Method

Another way of doing aggregations is by using the Mongo.Collection#rawCollection()
This can only be run on the Server.
Here is an example you can use in Meteor 1.3 and higher:
```
Meteor.methods({ 'aggregateUsers'(someId) {

const collection = MyCollection.rawCollection()

const aggregate = Meteor.wrapAsync(collection.aggregate, collection)
const match = { age: { $gte: 25 } }

const group = { _id:'$age', totalUsers: { $sum: 1 } }
const results = aggregate([
```

```
{ $match: match }, { $group: group }
])
return results

}
})
```

Section 5.12: Java and Spring example
This is an example code to create and execute the aggregate query in MongoDB using Spring Data.
```
try {
MongoClient mongo = new MongoClient(); DB db = mongo.getDB("so");
DBCollection coll = db.getCollection("employees");

//Equivalent to $match
DBObject matchFields = new BasicDBObject(); matchFields.put("dept", "Admin");
DBObject match = new BasicDBObject("$match", matchFields);

//Equivalent to $project
DBObject projectFields = new BasicDBObject(); projectFields.put("_id", 1); projectFields.put("name", 1); projectFields.put("dept", 1);
projectFields.put("totalExp", 1); projectFields.put("age", 1); projectFields.put("languages", 1);

DBObject project = new BasicDBObject("$project", projectFields);

//Equivalent to $group
DBObject groupFields = new BasicDBObject("_id", "$dept"); groupFields.put("ageSet", new BasicDBObject("$addToSet", "$age"));
DBObject employeeDocProjection = new BasicDBObject("$addToSet", new

BasicDBObject("totalExp",      "$totalExp").append("age",      "$age").append("languages",      "$languages").append("dept",
"$dept").append("name", "$name"));

groupFields.put("docs", employeeDocProjection);

DBObject group = new BasicDBObject("$group", groupFields);

//Sort results by age
DBObject sort = new BasicDBObject("$sort", new BasicDBObject("age", 1));
List<DBObject>   aggregationList   =   new   ArrayList<>();   aggregationList.add(match);   aggregationList.add(project);
aggregationList.add(group); aggregationList.add(sort);

AggregationOutput output = coll.aggregate(aggregationList);
for (DBObject result : output.results()) {

BasicDBList   employeeList   =   (BasicDBList)   result.get("docs");   BasicDBObject   employeeDoc   =   (BasicDBObject)
employeeList.get(0); String name = employeeDoc.get("name").toString(); System.out.println(name);
}
}catch (Exception ex){ ex.printStackTrace();
}
```
See the "resultSet" value in JSON format to understand the output format:
```
[{
"_id": "Admin", "ageSet": [35.0, 30.0], "docs": [{
"totalExp": 11.0, "age": 35.0,
"languages": ["english", "hindi"], "dept": "Admin",
"name": "Anna"
}, {
"totalExp": 10.0, "age": 30.0,
"languages": ["german", "french", "english", "hindi"], "dept": "Admin",
"name": "Adma"
}]
}]
```

The "resultSet" contains one entry for each group, "ageSet" contains the list of age of each employee of that group, "_id" contains the value of the field that is being used for grouping and "docs" contains data of each employee of that group that can be used in our own code and UI.

Chapter 6: Indexes

Section 6.1: Index Creation Basics

See the below transactions collection.
db.transactions.insert({ cr_dr : "D", amount : 100, fee : 2});
db.transactions.insert({ cr_dr : "C", amount : 100, fee : 2});
db.transactions.insert({ cr_dr : "C", amount : 10, fee : 2});
db.transactions.insert({ cr_dr : "D", amount : 100, fee : 4});
db.transactions.insert({ cr_dr : "D", amount : 10, fee : 2});
db.transactions.insert({ cr_dr : "C", amount : 10, fee : 4});
db.transactions.insert({ cr_dr : "D", amount : 100, fee : 2});
getIndexes() functions will show all the indices available for a collection.
db.transactions.getIndexes();

Let see the output of above statement.
[
{
"v" : 1, "key" : {
"_id" : 1
},
"name" : "_id_",
"ns" : "documentation_db.transactions"
}
]

There is already one index for transaction collection. This is because MongoDB creates a *unique index* on the _id field during the creation of a collection. The _id index prevents clients from inserting two documents with the same value for the _id field. You cannot drop this index on the _id field.

Now let's add an index for cr_dr field;
db.transactions.createIndex({ cr_dr : 1 });

The result of the index execution is as follows.
{
"createdCollectionAutomatically" : **false**, "numIndexesBefore" : 1, "numIndexesAfter" : 2,
"ok" : 1
}

The createdCollectionAutomatically indicates if the operation created a collection. If a collection does not exist, MongoDB creates the collection as part of the indexing operation.
Let run db.transactions.getIndexes(); again.
[
{
"v" : 1, "key" : {
"_id" : 1
},
"name" : "_id_",
"ns" : "documentation_db.transactions"
},
{
"v" : 1, "key" : {
"cr_dr" : 1
},
"name" : "cr_dr_1",
"ns" : "documentation_db.transactions"
}
]

Now you see transactions collection have two indices. Default _id index and cr_dr_1 which we created. The name is assigned by MongoDB. You can set your own name like below.
db.transactions.createIndex({ cr_dr : -1 },{name : "index on cr_dr desc"})
Now db.transactions.getIndexes(); will give you three indices.
[
{
"v" : 1, "key" : {
_id" : 1
},
"name" : "_id_",
"ns" : "documentation_db.transactions"
},
{
"v" : 1, "key" : {

```
"cr_dr" : 1
},
"name" : "cr_dr_1",
"ns" : "documentation_db.transactions"
},
{
"v" : 1, "key" : {
"cr_dr" : -1
},
"name" : "index on cr_dr desc",
"ns" : "documentation_db.transactions"
}
]
```

While creating index { cr_dr : -1 } 1 means index will be in ascending order and -1 for descending order.
Version ≥ 2.4

Hashed indexes
Indexes can be defined also as *hashed*. This is more performant on *equality queries*, but is not e cient for *range queries*; however you can define both hashed and ascending/descending indexes on the same field.
```
db.transactions.createIndex({ cr_dr : "hashed" });
db.transactions.getIndexes(
[
{
"v" : 1, "key" : {
"_id" : 1
},
"name" : "_id_",
"ns" : "documentation_db.transactions"
},
{
"v" : 1, "key" : {
"cr_dr" : "hashed"
},
"name" : "cr_dr_hashed",
"ns" : "documentation_db.transactions"
}
]
```

Section 6.2: Dropping/Deleting an Index
If index name is known,
db.collection.dropIndex('name_of_index');

If index name is not known,
db.collection.dropIndex({ 'name_of_field' : -1 });

Section 6.3: Sparse indexes and Partial indexes

Sparse indexes:
These can be particularly useful for fields that are optional but which should also be unique.
{ "_id" : "john@example.com", "nickname" : "Johnnie" } { "_id" : "jane@example.com" }
{ "_id" : "julia@example.com", "nickname" : "Jules"} { "_id" : "jack@example.com" }

Since two entries have no "nickname" specified and indexing will treat unspecified fields as null, the index creation would fail with 2 documents having 'null', so:
db.scores.createIndex({ nickname: 1 }, { unique: **true**, sparse: **true** })
will let you still have 'null' nicknames.

Sparse indexes are more compact since they skip/ignore documents that don't specify that field. So if you have a collection where only less than 10% of documents specify this field, you can create much smaller indexes - making better use of limited memory if you want to do queries like:
db.scores.find({'nickname': 'Johnnie'})

Partial indexes:
Partial indexes represent a superset of the functionality o ered by sparse indexes and should be preferred over sparse indexes. (*New in version 3.2*)
Partial indexes determine the index entries based on the specified filter.

db.restaurants.createIndex(
{ cuisine: 1 },
{ partialFilterExpression: { rating: { $gt: 5 } } }

)

If rating is greater than 5, then cuisine will be indexed. Yes, we can specify a property to be indexed based on the value of other properties also.

Difference between Sparse and Partial Indexes:
Sparse indexes select documents to index solely based on the existence of the indexed field, or for compound indexes, the existence of the indexed fields.
Partial indexes determine the index entries based on the specified filter. The filter can include fields other than the index keys and can specify conditions other than just an existence check. Still, a partial index can implement the same behavior as a sparse index
Eg:
db.contacts.createIndex(
{ name: 1 },
{ partialFilterExpression: { name: { $exists: **true** } } }
)

Note: Both the *partialFilterExpression* option and the *sparse* option cannot be specified at the same time.

Section 6.4: Get Indices of a Collection
db.collection.getIndexes();
Output
[
{
"v" : 1, "key" : {
"_id" : 1
},
"name" : "_id_",
"ns" : "documentation_db.transactions"
},
{
"v" : 1, "key" : {
"cr_dr" : 1
},
"name" : "cr_dr_1",
"ns" : "documentation_db.transactions"
},
{
"v" : 1, "key" : {
"cr_dr" : -1
},
"name" : "index on cr_dr desc",
"ns" : "documentation_db.transactions"
}
]

Section 6.5: Compound
db.people.createIndex({name: 1, age: -1})
This creates an index on multiple fields, in this case on the name and age fields. It will be ascending in name and descending in age.
In this type of index, the sort order is relevant, because it will determine whether the index can support a sort operation or not. Reverse sorting is supported on any prefix of a compound index, as long as the sort is in the reverse sort direction for **all** of the keys in the sort. Otherwise, sorting for compound indexes need to match the order of the index.

Field order is also important, in this case the index will be sorted first by name, and within each name value, sorted by the values of the age field. This allows the index to be used by queries on the name field, or on name and age, but not on age alone.

Section 6.6: Unique Index
db.collection.createIndex({ "user_id": 1 }, { unique: **true** })
enforce uniqueness on the defined index (either single or compound). Building the index will fail if the collection already contains duplicate values; the indexing will fail also with multiple entries missing the field (since they will all be indexed with the value **null**) unless sparse: **true** is specified.

Section 6.7: Single field
db.people.createIndex({name: 1})

This creates an ascending single field index on the field *name*.
In this type of indexes the sort order is irrelevant, because mongo can traverse the index in both directions.

Section 6.8: Delete
To drop an index you could use the index name
db.people.dropIndex("nameIndex")
Or the index specification document
db.people.dropIndex({name: 1})

Section 6.9: List
db.people.getIndexes()
This will return an array of documents each describing an index on the *people* collection

Section 6.10: Map-Reduce
As per the MongoDB documentation, **Map-reduce** is a data processing paradigm for condensing large volumes of data into useful aggregated results. MongoDB uses **mapReduce** command for map-reduce operations. MapReduce is generally used for processing large data sets.

MapReduce Command
Following is the syntax of the basic mapReduce command −

```
>db.collection.mapReduce(
   function() {emit(key,value);}, //map function
   function(key,values) {return reduceFunction}, {   //reduce function
      out: collection,
      query: document,
      sort: document,
      limit: number
   }
)
```

The map-reduce function first queries the collection, then maps the result documents to emit key-value pairs, which is then reduced based on the keys that have multiple values.
In the above syntax −
- **map** is a javascript function that maps a value with a key and emits a key-value pair
- **reduce** is a javascript function that reduces or groups all the documents having the same key
- **out** specifies the location of the map-reduce query result
- **query** specifies the optional selection criteria for selecting documents
- **sort** specifies the optional sort criteria
- **limit** specifies the optional maximum number of documents to be returned

Using MapReduce

Consider the following document structure storing user posts. The document stores user_name of the user and the status of post.

```
{
   "post_text": "tutorialspoint is an awesome website for tutorials",
   "user_name": "mark",
   "status":"active"
}
```

Now, we will use a mapReduce function on our **posts** collection to select all the active posts, group them on the basis of user_name and then count the number of posts by each user using the following code −

```
>db.posts.mapReduce(
```

```
function() { emit(this.user_id,1); },

function(key, values) {return Array.sum(values)}, {
  query:{status:"active"},
  out:"post_total"
  }
)
```

The above mapReduce query outputs the following result -

```
{
  "result" : "post_total",
  "timeMillis" : 9,
  "counts" : {
    "input" : 4,
    "emit" : 4,
    "reduce" : 2,
    "output" : 2
  },
  "ok" : 1,
}
```

The result shows that a total of 4 documents matched the query (status:"active"), the map function emitted 4 documents with key-value pairs and finally the reduce function grouped mapped documents having the same keys into 2.

To see the result of this mapReduce query, use the find operator -

```
>db.posts.mapReduce(
  function() { emit(this.user_id,1); },
  function(key, values) {return Array.sum(values)}, {
    query:{status:"active"},
    out:"post_total"
  }
).find()
```

The above query gives the following result which indicates that both users **tom** and **mark** have two posts in active states -

```
{ "_id" : "tom", "value" : 2 }
{ "_id" : "mark", "value" : 2 }
```

In a similar manner, MapReduce queries can be used to construct large complex aggregation queries. The use of custom Javascript functions make use of MapReduce which is very flexible and powerful.

Chapter 7:
Bulk Operations &2dsphere Index

Section 7.1: Converting a field to another type and updating the entire collection in Bulk

Usually the case when one wants to change a field type to another, for instance the original collection may have

"numerical" or "date" fields saved as strings:
```
{
"name": "Alice", "salary": "57871", "dob": "1986-08-21"
},
{
"name": "Bob", "salary": "48974", "dob": "1990-11-04"
}
```

The objective would be to update a humongous collection like the above to
```
{
"name": "Alice", "salary": 57871,

"dob": ISODate("1986-08-21T00:00:00.000Z")

},

{

"name": "Bob", "salary": 48974,

"dob": ISODate("1990-11-04T00:00:00.000Z")

}
```

For relatively small data, one can achieve the above by iterating the collection using a snapshot with the cursor's forEach() method and updating each document as follows:

db.test.find({

"salary": { "$exists": **true**, "$type": 2 }, "dob": { "$exists": **true**, "$type": 2 }

}).snapshot().forEach(**function**(doc){

var   newSalary = parseInt(doc.salary), newDob = **new** ISODate(doc.dob);

db.test.updateOne(

{ "_id": doc._id },

{ "$set": { "salary": newSalary, "dob": newDob } }

);

});

Whilst this is optimal for small collections, performance with large collections is greatly reduced since looping through a large dataset and sending each update operation per request to the server incurs a computational penalty.

The Bulk() API comes to the rescue and greatly improves performance since write operations are sent to the server only once in bulk. E ciency is achieved since the method does not send every write request to the server (as with the current update statement within the forEach() loop) but just once in every 1000 requests, thus making updates more e cient and quicker than currently is.

Using the same concept above with the forEach() loop to create the batches, we can update the collection in bulk as follows. In this demonstration the Bulk() API available in MongoDB versions >= 2.6 and < 3.2 uses the initializeUnorderedBulkOp() method to execute in parallel, as well as in a nondeterministic order, the write operations in the batches.

It updates all the documents in the clients collection by changing the salary and dob fields to numerical and datetime values respectively:
var bulk = db.test.initializeUnorderedBulkOp(),

counter = 0; // counter to keep track of the batch update size
db.test.find({

"salary": { "$exists": **true**, "$type": 2 }, "dob": { "$exists": **true**, "$type": 2 }

}).snapshot().forEach(**function**(doc){

```
var         newSalary = parseInt(doc.salary), newDob = new ISODate(doc.dob);

bulk.find({ "_id": doc._id }).updateOne({

"$set": { "salary": newSalary, "dob": newDob }

});

counter++; // increment counter If (counter % 1000 == 0)
{

bulk.execute(); // Execute per 1000 operations and re-initialize every 1000 update statements
bulk = db.test.initializeUnorderedBulkOp();

}

});
```

The next example applies to the new MongoDB version 3.2 which has since deprecated the Bulk() API and provided a newer set of apis using bulkWrite().
It uses the same cursors as above but creates the arrays with the bulk operations using the same forEach() cursor method to push each bulk write document to the array. Because write commands can accept no more than 1000 operations, there's need to group operations to have at most 1000 operations and re-intialise the array when the loop hits the 1000 iteration:

```
var cursor = db.test.find({

"salary": { "$exists": true, "$type": 2 }, "dob": { "$exists": true, "$type": 2 }

}),

bulkUpdateOps = [];
cursor.snapshot().forEach(function(doc){ var newSalary = parseInt(doc.salary),

newDob = new ISODate(doc.dob); bulkUpdateOps.push({

"updateOne": {

"filter": { "_id": doc._id },

"update": { "$set": { "salary": newSalary, "dob": newDob } }

}

});

If (bulkUpdateOps.length === 1000) { db.test.bulkWrite(bulkUpdateOps); bulkUpdateOps = [];

}

});

If (bulkUpdateOps.length > 0) { db.test.bulkWrite(bulkUpdateOps); }
```

Section 7.2: Create a 2dsphere Index

db.collection.createIndex() method is used to create a 2dsphere index. The blueprint of a 2dsphere index :
db.collection.createIndex({ <location field> : "2dsphere" })

Here, the location field is the key and 2dsphere is the type of the index. In the following example we are going to create a 2dsphre index in the places collection.
db.places.insert(

{

loc : { type: "Point", coordinates: [-73.97, 40.77] }, name: "Central Park",
category : "Parks"

})

The following operation will create 2dsphere index on the loc field of places collection.
db.places.createIndex({ loc : "2dsphere" })

Chapter 8:
Pluggable Storage Engines

Section 8.1: WiredTiger

WiredTiger supports **LSM trees to store indexes**. LSM trees are faster for write operations when you need to write huge workloads of random inserts.

In WiredTiger, there is **no in-place updates**. If you need to update an element of a document, a new document will be inserted while the old document will be deleted.

WiredTiger also o ers **document-level concurrency**. It assumes that two write operations will not a ect the same document, but if it does, one operation will be rewind and executed later. That's a great performance boost if

rewinds are rare.
WiredTiger supports **Snappy and zLib algorithms for compression** of data and indexes in the file system. Snappy is the default. It is less CPU-intensive but have a lower compression rate than zLib.

How to use WiredTiger Engine

mongod --storageEngine wiredTiger --dbpath <newWiredTigerDBPath>
Note:
After mongodb 3.2, the default engine is WiredTiger.

newWiredTigerDBPath should not contain data of another storage engine. To migrate your data, you have to dump them, and re-import them in the new storage engine.

mongodump --out <exportDataDestination>

mongod --storageEngine wiredTiger --dbpath <newWiredTigerDBPath> mongorestore <exportDataDestination>

Section 8.2: MMAP

MMAP is a pluggable storage engine that was named after the mmap() Linux command. It maps files to the virtual memory and optimizes read calls. If you have a large file but needs to read just a small part of it, mmap() is much faster then a read() call that would bring entire file to the memory.

One disadvantage is that you can't have two write calls being processed in parallel for the same collection. So, MMAP has collection-level locking (and not document-level locking as WiredTiger o ers). This collection-locking is necessary because one MMAP index can reference multiples documents and if those docs could be updated simultaneously, the index would be inconsistent.

Section 8.3: In-memory
All data is stored in-memory (RAM) for faster read/access.

Section 8.4: mongo-rocks
A key-value engine created to integrate with Facebook's RocksDB.

Section 8.5: Fusion-io
A storage engine created by SanDisk that makes it possible to bypass the OS file system layer and write directly to the storage device.

Section 8.6: TokuMX

A storage engine created by Percona that uses fractal tree indexes.

Chapter 9: Connetivity

Java Driver
Section 9.1: Fetch Collection data with condition
To get data from testcollection collection in testdb database where name=dev

import org.bson.Document;

import com.mongodb.BasicDBObject; import com.mongodb.MongoClient; import com.mongodb.ServerAddress;

```java
import com.mongodb.client.MongoCollection; import com.mongodb.client.MongoCursor; import com.mongodb.client.MongoDatabase;

MongoClient mongoClient = new MongoClient(new ServerAddress("localhost", 27017));
MongoDatabase db = mongoClient.getDatabase("testdb");

MongoCollection<Document> collection = db.getCollection("testcollection");

BasicDBObject searchQuery = new BasicDBObject(); searchQuery.put("name","dev");

MongoCursor<Document> cursor = collection.find(searchQuery).iterator(); try {
while (cursor.hasNext()) { System.out.println(cursor.next().toJson());

}

} finally { cursor.close();
}
```

Section 9.2: Create a database user
To create a user **dev** with password **password123**
```java
MongoClient mongo = new MongoClient("localhost", 27017);
MongoDatabase db = mongo.getDatabase("testDB");
Map<String, Object> commandArguments = new BasicDBObject();
commandArguments.put("createUser", "dev"); commandArguments.put("pwd", "password123");
String[] roles = { "readWrite" }; commandArguments.put("roles", roles);
BasicDBObject command = new BasicDBObject(commandArguments); db.runCommand(command);
```

Section 9.3: Create a tailable cursor
find(query).projection(fields).cursorType(CursorType.TailableAwait).iterator();
That code applies to the MongoCollection class.
CursorType is an enum and it has the following values:
Tailable
TailableAwait

Corresponding to the old (<3.0) DBCursor addOption Bytes types:

Bytes.QUERYOPTION_TAILABLE

Bytes.QUERYOPTION_AWAITDATA

Python Driver
Section 9.4: Connect to MongoDB using pymongo
```python
from pymongo import MongoClient
uri = "mongodb://localhost:27017/"
client = MongoClient(uri)
db = client['test_db']
```

or

```python
db = client.test_db
collection = db['test_collection']
```

or

```python
collection = db.test_collection
collection.save({"hello":"world"})
print collection.find_one()
```

Section 9.5: PyMongo queries
Once you got a collection object, queries use the same syntax as in the mongo shell. Some slight di erences are: every key must be enclosed in brackets. For example:

db.find({frequencies: {$exists: **true**}})
becomes in pymongo (note the True in uppercase):

db.find({"frequencies": { "$exists": True }})

objects such as object ids or ISODate are manipulated using python classes. PyMongo uses its own ObjectId class to deal with object ids, while dates use the standard datetime package. For example, if you want to query all events between 2010 and 2011, you can do:
from datetime import datetime
date_from = datetime(2010, 1, 1) date_to = datetime(2011, 1, 1)

db.find({ "date": { "$gte": date_from, "$lt": date_to } }):

Section 9.6: Update all documents in a collection using PyMongo
Let's say you need to add a field to every document in a collection.
import pymongo
client = pymongo.MongoClient('localhost', 27017) db = client.mydb.mycollection
for doc in db.find(): db.update(

{'_id': doc['_id']},

{'$set': {'newField': 10} }, upsert=False, multi=False)

The find method returns a Cursor, on which you can easily iterate over using the **for in** syntax. Then, we call the update method, specifying the _id and that we add a field ($set). The parameters upsert and multi come from mongodb

PHP Driver
Section 9.8: Connect to MongoDB With PHP
To use MongoDB with PHP, you need to use MongoDB PHP driver. Download the driver from the url
https://s3.amazonaws.com/drivers.mongodb.org/php/index.html.
Make sure to download the latest release of it. Now unzip the archive and put php_mongo.dll in your PHP extension directory ("ext" by default) and add the following line to your php.ini file –

extension = php_mongo.dll

Make a Connection and Select a Database
To make a connection, you need to specify the database name, if the database doesn't exist then MongoDB creates it automatically.
Following is the code snippet to connect to the database –

```
<?php
   // connect to mongodb
   $m = new MongoClient();
   echo "Connection to database successfully";
   // select a database
   $db = $m->mydb;
   echo "Database mydb selected";
?>
```

When the program is executed, it will produce the following result –

Connection to database successfully
Database mydb selected

Create a Collection
Following is the code snippet to create a collection –

```
<?php
   // connect to mongodb
   $m = new MongoClient();
   echo "Connection to database successfully";
   // select a database
   $db = $m->mydb;
   echo "Database mydb selected";
```

```php
$collection = $db->createCollection("mycol");
echo "Collection created succsessfully";
?>
```

When the program is executed, it will produce the following result −

```
Connection to database successfully
Database mydb selected
Collection created succsessfully
```

Insert a Document

To insert a document into MongoDB, **insert()** method is used.
Following is the code snippet to insert a document −

```php
<?php
   // connect to mongodb
   $m = new MongoClient();
   echo "Connection to database successfully";
   // select a database
   $db = $m->mydb;
   echo "Database mydb selected";
   $collection = $db->mycol;
   echo "Collection selected succsessfully";
   $document = array( 
      "title" => "MongoDB", 
      "description" => "database", 
      "likes" => 100,
      "url" => "http://www.tutorialspoint.com/mongodb/",
      "by" => "tutorials point"
   );
   $collection->insert($document);
   echo "Document inserted successfully";
?>
```

When the program is executed, it will produce the following result −

```
Connection to database successfully
Database mydb selected
Collection selected succsessfully
Document inserted successfully
```

Find All Documents

To select all documents from the collection, find() method is used.
Following is the code snippet to select all documents −

```php
<?php
   // connect to mongodb
   $m = new MongoClient();
   echo "Connection to database successfully";
   // select a database
   $db = $m->mydb;
   echo "Database mydb selected";
   $collection = $db->mycol;
   echo "Collection selected succsessfully";
   $cursor = $collection->find();
   // iterate cursor to display title of documents
   foreach ($cursor as $document) {
      echo $document["title"] . "\n";
   }
?>
```

When the program is executed, it will produce the following result −

```
Connection to database successfully
Database mydb selected
Collection selected succsessfully {
  "title": "MongoDB"
}
```

Update a Document

To update a document, you need to use the update() method.
In the following example, we will update the title of inserted document to **MongoDB Tutorial**.
Following is the code snippet to update a document −

```
<?php
  // connect to mongodb
  $m = new MongoClient();
  echo "Connection to database successfully";
  // select a database
  $db = $m->mydb;
  echo "Database mydb selected";
  $collection = $db->mycol;
  echo "Collection selected succsessfully";
  // now update the document
  $collection->update(array("title"=>"MongoDB"),
    array('$set'=>array("title"=>"MongoDB Tutorial")));
  echo "Document updated successfully";
  // now display the updated document
  $cursor = $collection->find();
  // iterate cursor to display title of documents
  echo "Updated document";
  foreach ($cursor as $document) {
    echo $document["title"] . "\n";
  }
?>
```

When the program is executed, it will produce the following result −

```
Connection to database successfully
Database mydb selected
Collection selected succsessfully
Document updated successfully
Updated document {
  "title": "MongoDB Tutorial"
}
```

Delete a Document

To delete a document, you need to use remove() method.
In the following example, we will remove the documents that has the title **MongoDB Tutorial**.
Following is the code snippet to delete a document −

```
<?php
  // connect to mongodb
  $m = new MongoClient();
  echo "Connection to database successfully";
  // select a database
  $db = $m->mydb;
  echo "Database mydb selected";
  $collection = $db->mycol;
  echo "Collection selected succsessfully";
  // now remove the document
  $collection->remove(array("title"=>"MongoDB Tutorial"),false);
```

```
  echo "Documents deleted successfully";
  // now display the available documents
  $cursor = $collection->find();
  // iterate cursor to display title of documents
  echo "Updated document";
  foreach ($cursor as $document) {
     echo $document["title"] . "\n";
  }
?>
```

When the program is executed, it will produce the following result -

```
Connection to database successfully
Database mydb selected
Collection selected succsessfully
Documents deleted successfully
```

In the above example, the second parameter is boolean type and used for **justOne** field of **remove()** method.
Remaining MongoDB methods **findOne()**, **save()**, **limit()**, **skip()**, **sort()** etc. works same as explained above.

Chapter 10: Mongo as Shards

Section 10.1: Sharding Environment Setup

Sharding Group Members :
For sharding there are three players.
    Config Server
    Replica Sets
    Mongos

For a mongo shard we need to setup the above three servers.
Config Server Setup : add the following to mongod conf file
sharding:

clusterRole: configsvr replication:

replSetName: <setname>
run : mongod --config

we can choose config server as replica set or may be a standalone server. Based on our requirement we can choose the best. If config need to run in replica set we need to follow the replica set setup

Replica Setup : Create replica set // Please refer the replica setup
MongoS Setup : Mongos is main setup in shard. Its is query router to access all replica sets
Add the following in mongos conf file
sharding:

configDB: <configReplSetName>/cfg1.example.net:27017;

Configure Shared :
Connect the mongos via shell (mongo --host --port)
sh.addShard("/s1-mongo1.example.net:27017")

sh.enableSharding("")

sh.shardCollection("< database >.< collection >", { < key > : < direction > })

sh.status() // To ensure the sharding

Chapter 11: Replication

Section 11.1: Basic configuration with three nodes
The replica set is a group of mongod instances that maintain the same data set.
This example shows how to configure a replica set with three instances on the same server.
Creating data folders
mkdir /srv/mongodb/data/rs0-0 mkdir /srv/mongodb/data/rs0-1 mkdir /srv/mongodb/data/rs0-2
Starting mongod instances
mongod --port 27017 --dbpath /srv/mongodb/data/rs0-0 --replSet rs0 mongod --port 27018 --dbpath /srv/mongodb/data/rs0-1 --replSet rs0 mongod --port 27019 --dbpath /srv/mongodb/data/rs0-2 --replSet rs0

Configuring replica set
mongo --port 27017   // *connection to the instance 27017*
rs.initiate(); rs.add("<hostname>:27018") rs.add("<hostname>:27019")
initilization of replica set on the 1st node
adding a 2nd node
adding a 3rd node

Testing your setup

For checking the configuration type rs.status(), the result should be like:
{
"set" : "rs0",
"date" : ISODate("2016-09-01T12:34:24.968Z"), "myState" : 1,
"term" : NumberLong(4), "heartbeatIntervalMillis" : NumberLong(2000), "members" : [
{
"_id" : 0,
"name" : "<hostname>:27017", "health" : 1,
"state" : 1, "stateStr" : "PRIMARY",
....
},
{
"_id" : 1,
"name" : "<hostname>:27018", "health" : 1,
"state" : 2,
"stateStr" : "SECONDARY",
},
{

"_id" : 2,
"name" : "<hostname>:27019",
"health" : 1, "state" : 2,
"stateStr" : "SECONDARY",
....
}
],
"ok" : 1
}

Mongo as a Replica Set
Section 11.2: Mongodb as a Replica Set
We would be creating mongodb as a replica set having 3 instances. One instance would be primary and the other 2 instances would be secondary.
For simplicity, I am going to have a replica set with 3 instances of mongodb running on the same server and thus to achieve this, all three mongodb instances would be running on di erent port numbers.

In production environment where in you have a dedicated mongodb instance running on a single server you can reuse the same port numbers.

Create data directories (path where mongodb data would be stored in a file)
mkdir c:\data\server1 (datafile path **for** instance 1)

mkdir c:\data\server2 (datafile path **for** instance 2)

mkdir c:\data\server3 (datafile path **for** instance 3)

2. a Start the first mongod instance
    Open command prompt and type the following press enter.
mongod --replSet s0 --dbpath c:\data\server1 --port 37017 --smallfiles --oplogSize 100
The above command associates the instance of mongodb to a replicaSet name "s0" and the starts the first instance of mongodb on port 37017 with oplogSize 100MB

2. b. Similarly start the second instance of Mongodb
mongod --replSet s0 --dbpath c:\data\server2 --port 37018 --smallfiles --oplogSize 100
The above command associates the instance of mongodb to a replicaSet name "s0" and the starts the first instance of mongodb on port 37018 with oplogSize 100MB

2. c. Now start the third instance of Mongodb
mongod --replSet s0 --dbpath c:\data\server3 --port 37019 --smallfiles --oplogSize 100
The above command associates the instance of mongodb to a replicaSet name "s0" and the starts the first instance of mongodb on port 37019 with oplogSize 100MB
With all the 3 instances started, these 3 instances are independent of each other currently. We would now need to group these instances as a replica set. We do this with the help of a config object.

3.a Connect to any of the mongod servers via the mongo shell. To do that open the command prompt and type.
mongo --port 37017
Once connected to the mongo shell, create a config object
var config = {"_id":"s0", members[]};
this config object has 2 attributes
_id: the name of the replica Set ("s0")
members: [] (members is an array of mongod instances. lets keep this blank for now, we will add members via the push command.

3.b To Push(add) mongod instances to the members array in the config object. On the mongo shell type
config.members.push({"_id":0,"host":"localhost:37017"});   config.members.push({"_id":1,"host":"localhost:37018"});
config.members.push({"_id":2,"host":"localhost:37019"});

We assign each mongod instance an _id and an host. _id can be any unique number and the host should be the hostname of the server on which its running followed by the port number.

4. Initiate the config object by the following command in the mongo shell.
rs.initiate(config)

Give it a few seconds and we have a replica set of 3 mongod instances running on the server. type the following command to check the status of the replica set and to identify which one is primary and which one is secondary.
rs.status();

Section 11.3: Check MongoDB Replica Set states
Use the below command to check the replica set status.
Command : rs.status()
Connect any one of replica member and fire this command it will give the full state of the replica set
Example :
{
"set" : "ReplicaName",
"date" : ISODate("2016-09-26T07:36:04.935Z"), "myState" : 1,
"term" : NumberLong(-1), "heartbeatIntervalMillis" : NumberLong(2000), "members" : [
{
"_id" : 0,
"name" : "<IP>:<PORT>", "health" : 1,
"state" : 1, "stateStr" : "PRIMARY", "uptime" : 5953744,
"optime"   :   Timestamp(1474875364,   36),   "optimeDate"   :   ISODate("2016-09-26T07:36:04Z"),   "electionTime"   :
Timestamp(1468921646, 1), "electionDate" : ISODate("2016-07-19T09:47:26Z"), "configVersion" : 6,
"self" : true
},
{
"_id" : 1,
"name" : "<IP>:<PORT>", "health" : 1,
"state" : 2,
"stateStr" : "SECONDARY", "uptime" : 5953720,
"optime" : Timestamp(1474875364, 13), "optimeDate" : ISODate("2016-09-26T07:36:04Z"),

```
"lastHeartbeat" : ISODate("2016-09-26T07:36:04.244Z"), "lastHeartbeatRecv" : ISODate("2016-09-26T07:36:03.871Z"), "pingMs" :
NumberLong(0),
"syncingTo" : "10.9.52.55:10050", "configVersion" : 6
},
{
"_id" : 2,
"name" : "<IP>:<PORT>", "health" : 1,
"state" : 7, "stateStr" : "ARBITER", "uptime" : 5953696,
"lastHeartbeat" : ISODate("2016-09-26T07:36:03.183Z"), "lastHeartbeatRecv" : ISODate("2016-09-26T07:36:03.715Z"), "pingMs" :
NumberLong(0),
"configVersion" : 6
},
{
"_id" : 3,
"name" : "<IP>:<PORT>", "health" : 1,
"state" : 2,
"stateStr" : "SECONDARY", "uptime" : 1984305,
"optime" : Timestamp(1474875361, 16), "optimeDate" : ISODate("2016-09-26T07:36:01Z"),
"lastHeartbeat" : ISODate("2016-09-26T07:36:02.921Z"), "lastHeartbeatRecv" : ISODate("2016-09-26T07:36:03.793Z"), "pingMs" :
NumberLong(22),
"lastHeartbeatMessage" : "syncing from: 10.9.52.56:10050", "syncingTo" : "10.9.52.56:10050",
"configVersion" : 6
}
],
"ok" : 1
}
```

From the above we can know the entire replica set status

MongoDB - Configure a ReplicaSet to support TLS/SSL

How to configure a ReplicaSet to support TLS/SSL?
We will deploy a 3 Nodes ReplicaSet in your local environment and we will use a self-signed certificate. Do not use a self-signed certificate in PRODUCTION.

How to connect your Client to this ReplicaSet?
We will connect a Mongo Shell.
A description of TLS/SSL, PKI (Public Key Infrastructure) certificates, and Certificate Authority is beyond the scope of this documentation.

Section 11.4: How to configure a ReplicaSet to support TLS/SSL?

Create the Root Certificate
The Root Certificate (aka CA File) will be used to sign and identify your certificate. To generate it, run the command below.
openssl req -nodes -out ca.pem -**new** -x509 -keyout ca.key
Keep the root certificate and its key carefully, both will be used to sign your certificates. The root certificate might be used by your client as well.

Generate the Certificate Requests and the Private Keys
When generating the Certificate Signing Request (aka CSR), **input the exact hostname (or IP) of your node in the Common Name (aka CN) field. The others fields must have exactly the same value.** You might need to modify your /etc/hosts file.

The commands below will generate the CSR files and the RSA Private Keys (4096 bits).
openssl req -nodes -newkey rsa:4096 -sha256 -keyout mongodb_node_1.key -out mongodb_node_1.csr openssl req -nodes -newkey rsa:4096 -sha256 -keyout mongodb_node_2.key -out mongodb_node_2.csr openssl req -nodes -newkey rsa:4096 -sha256 -keyout mongodb_node_3.key -out mongodb_node_3.csr

You must generate one CSR for each node of your ReplicaSet. Remember that the Common Name is not the same from one node to another. Don't base multiple CSRs on the same Private Key.

You must now have 3 CSRs and 3 Private Keys.

mongodb_node_1.key - mongodb_node_2.key - mongodb_node_3.key mongodb_ncde_1.csr - mongodb_node_2.csr - mongodb_node_3.csr

Sign your Certificate Requests

Use the CA File (ca.pem) and its Private Key (ca.key) generated previously to sign each Certificate Request by running the commands below.
openssl x509 -req -in mongodb_node_1.csr -CA ca.pem -CAkey ca.key -set_serial 00 -out mongodb_node_1.crt
openssl x509 -req -in mongodb_node_2.csr -CA ca.pem -CAkey ca.key -set_serial 00 -out mongodb_node_2.crt
openssl x509 -req -in mongodb_node_3.csr -CA ca.pem -CAkey ca.key -set_serial 00 -out mongodb_node_3.crt

You must sign each CSR.
Your must now have 3 CSRs, 3 Private Keys and 3 self-signed Certificates. Only the Private Keys and the Certificates will be used by MongoDB.
mongodb_node_1.key - mongodb_node_2.key - mongodb_node_3.key mongodb_node_1.csr - mongodb_node_2.csr - mongodb_node_3.csr mongodb_node_1.crt - mongodb_node_2.crt - mongodb_node_3.crt
Each certificate corresponds to one node. Remember carefully which CN / hostname your gave to each CSR.

Concat each Node Certificate with its key

Run the commands below to concat each Node Certificate with its key in one file (MongoDB requirement).
cat mongodb_node_1.key mongodb_node_1.crt > mongodb_node_1.pem cat mongodb_node_2.key mongodb_node_2.crt > mongodb_node_2.pem cat mongodb_node_3.key mongodb_node_3.crt > mongodb_node_3.pem

Your must now have 3 PEM files.
mongodb_node_1.pem - mongodb_node_2.pem - mongodb_node_3.pem

Deploy your ReplicaSet
We will assume that your pem files are located in your current folder as well as data/data1, data/data2 and data/data3.
Run the commands below to deploy your 3 Nodes ReplicaSet listening on port 27017, 27018 and 27019.
mongod --dbpath data/data_1 --replSet rs0 --port 27017 --sslMode requireSSL --sslPEMKeyFile mongodb_node_1.pem
mongod --dbpath data/data_2 --replSet rs0 --port 27018 --sslMode requireSSL --sslPEMKeyFile mongodb_node_2.pem
mongod --dbpath data/data_3 --replSet rs0 --port 27019 --sslMode requireSSL --sslPEMKeyFile mongodb_node_3.pem

You now have a 3 Nodes ReplicaSet deployed on your local environment and all their transactions are encrypted. You cannot connect to this ReplicaSet without using TLS.

Deploy your ReplicaSet for Mutual SSL / Mutual Trust
To force your client to provide a Client Certificate (Mutual SSL), you must add the CA File when running your instances.
mongod --dbpath data/data_1 --replSet rs0 --port 27017 --sslMode requireSSL --sslPEMKeyFile mongodb_node_1.pem --sslCAFile ca.pem

mongod --dbpath data/data_2 --replSet rs0 --port 27018 --sslMode requireSSL --sslPEMKeyFile mongodb_node_2.pem --sslCAFile ca.pem
mongod --dbpath data/data_3 --replSet rs0 --port 27019 --sslMode requireSSL --sslPEMKeyFile mongodb_node_3.pem --sslCAFile ca.pem

You now have a 3 Nodes ReplicaSet deployed on your local environment and all their transactions are encrypted. You cannot connect to this ReplicaSet without using TLS or without providing a Client Certificate trusted by your CA.

Section 11.5: How to connect your Client (Mongo Shell) to a ReplicaSet?

No Mutual SSL
In this example, we might use the CA File (ca.pem) that you generated during the "*How to configure a ReplicaSet to support TLS/SSL?*" section. We will assume that the CA file is located in your current folder.

We will assume that your 3 nodes are running on mongo1:27017, mongo2:27018 and mongo3:27019. (You might need to modify your */etc/hosts* file.)

From MongoDB 3.2.6, if your CA File is registered in your Operating System Trust Store, you can connect to your ReplicaSet without providing the CA File.

mongo --ssl --host rs0/mongo1:27017,mongo2:27018,mongo3:27019

Otherwise you must provide the CA File.
mongo --ssl --sslCAFile ca.pem --host rs0/mongo1:27017,mongo2:27018,mongo3:27019

You are now connected to your ReplicaSet and all the transactions between your Mongo Shell and your ReplicaSet are encrypted.

With Mutual SSL
If your ReplicaSet asks for a Client Certificate, you must provide one signed by the CA used by the ReplicaSet Deployment. The steps to generate the Client Certificate are almost the same as the ones to generate the Server Certificate.

Indeed, you just need to modify the Common Name Field during the CSR creation. Instead of providing 1 Node Hostname in the Common Name Field, **you need to provide all the ReplicaSet Hostnames separated by a comma**.
openssl req -nodes -newkey rsa:4096 -sha256 -keyout mongodb_client.key -out mongodb_client.csr

...

Common Name (e.g. server FQDN or YOUR name) []: mongo1,mongo2,mongo3

You might face the Common Name size limitation if the Common Name field is too long (more than 64 bytes long). To bypass this limitation, you must use the SubjectAltName when generating the CSR.
openssl req -nodes -newkey rsa:4096 -sha256 -keyout mongodb_client.key -out mongodb_client.csr - config <(
cat <<-EOF [req]

default_bits = 4096 prompt = no default_md = sha256

req_extensions = req_ext
distinguished_name = dn
[dn] CN = .
[req_ext]

subjectAltName = @alt_names
[alt_names] DNS.1 = mongo1 DNS.2 = mongo2 DNS.3 = mongo3 EOF

)

Then you sign the CSR using the CA certificate and key.
openssl x509 -req -in mongodb_client.csr -CA ca.pem -CAkey ca.key -set_serial 00 -out mongodb_client.crt

Finally, you concat the key and the signed certificate.
cat mongodb_client.key mongodb_client.crt > mongodb_client.pem

To connect to your ReplicaSet, you can now provide the newly generated Client Certificate.
mongo --ssl --sslCAFile ca.pem --host rs0/mongo1:27017,mongo2:27018,mongo3:27019 --sslPEMKeyFile mongodb_client.pem

You are now connected to your ReplicaSet and all the transactions between your Mongo Shell and your ReplicaSet are encrypted.

Chapter 12:
Authentication Mechanisms & Authorization Model in MongoDB

Authentication is the process of verifying the identity of a client. When access control, i.e. authorization, is enabled, MongoDB requires all clients to authenticate themselves in order to determine their access.

MongoDB supports a number of authentication mechanisms that clients can use to verify their identity. These mechanisms allow MongoDB to integrate into your existing authentication system.

Section 12.1: Authentication Mechanisms
MongoDB supports multiple authentication mechanisms.
Client and User Authentication Mechanisms
SCRAM-SHA-1
X.509 Certificate Authentication
MongoDB Challenge and Response (MONGODB-CR)
LDAP proxy authentication, and
Kerberos authentication

Internal Authentication Mechanisms
Keyfile

X.509

MongoDB Authorization Model
Authorization is the basically verifies user privileges. MongoDB support di erent kind of authorization models. 1. **Role base access control**
 Role are group of privileges, actions over resources. That are gain to users over a given namespace (Database). Actions are performs on resources. Resources are any object that hold state in database.

Section 12.2: Build-in Roles
Built-in database user roles and database administration roles roles exist in each database.
Database User Roles
read

readwrite

Chapter 13: Configuration

Parameter	Default
systemLog.verbosity	0
systemLog.quiet	false
systemLog.traceAllExceptions	false
systemLog.syslogFacility	user
systemLog.path	-
systemLog.logAppend	false
systemLog.logRotate	rename
systemLog.destination	stdout
systemLog.timeStampFormat	iso8601-local
systemLog.component.accessControl.verbosity	0
systemLog.component.command.verbosity	0
systemLog.component.control.verbosity	0
systemLog.component.ftdc.verbosity	0
systemLog.component.geo.verbosity	0
systemLog.component.index.verbosity	0
systemLog.component.network.verbo	0
systemLog.component.query.verbosity	0
systemLog.component.replication.verbosity	0
systemLog.component.sharding.verbosity	0
systemLog.component.storage.verbosity	0
systemLog.component.storage.journal.verbosity	0
systemLog.component.write.verbosity	0
processManagement.fork	false
processManagement.pidFilePath	none
net.port	27017
net.bindIp	0.0.0.0
net.maxIncomingConnections	65536
net.wireObjectCheck	true
net.ipv6	false
net.unixDomainSocket.enabled	true
net.unixDomainSocket.pathPrefix	/tmp
net.unixDomainSocket.filePermissions	0700
net.http.enabled	false
net.http.JSONPEnabled	false
net.http.RESTInterfaceEnabled	false
net.ssl.sslOnNormalPorts	false
net.ssl.mode	disabled
net.ssl.PEMKeyFile	none
net.ssl.PEMKeyPassword	none
net.ssl.clusterFile	none
net.ssl.clusterPassword	none
net.ssl.CAFile	none
net.ssl.CRLFile	none
net.ssl.allowConnectionsWithoutCertificates	false
net.ssl.allowInvalidCertificates	false
net.ssl.allowInvalidHostnames	false
net.ssl.disabledProtocols	none
net.ssl.FIPSMode	false

Section 13.1: Starting mongo with a specific config file

Using the --config flag.
$ /bin/mongod --config /etc/mongod.conf $ /bin/mongos --config /etc/mongos.conf

Note that -f is the shorter synonym for --config.

Chapter 14: Backing up and Restoring Data

Section 14.1: Basic mongodump of local default mongod instance

mongodump --db mydb --gzip --out "mydb.dump.$(date +%F_%R)"
This command will dump a bson gzipped archive of your local mongod 'mydb' database to the 'mydb.dump.{timestamp}' directory

Section 14.2: Basic mongorestore of local default mongod dump

mongorestore --db mydb mydb.dump.2016-08-27_12:44/mydb --drop --gzip
This command will first drop your current 'mydb' database and then restore your gzipped bson dump from the 'mydb mydb.dump.2016-08-27_12:44/mydb' archive dump file.

Section 14.3: mongoimport with JSON

Sample zipcode dataset in zipcodes.json stored in c:\Users\yc03ak1\Desktop\zips.json
{ "_id" : "01001", "city" : "AGAWAM", "loc" : [-72.622739, 42.070206], "pop" : 15338, "state" : "MA" }
{ "_id" : "01002", "city" : "CUSHMAN", "loc" : [-72.51564999999999, 42.377017], "pop" : 36963, "state" : "MA" }
{ "_id" : "01005", "city" : "BARRE", "loc" : [-72.10835400000001, 42.409698], "pop" : 4546, "state" : "MA" }
{ "_id" : "01007", "city" : "BELCHERTOWN", "loc" : [-72.41095300000001, 42.275103], "pop" : 10579, "state" : "MA" }
{ "_id" : "01008", "city" : "BLANDFORD", "loc" : [-72.936114, 42.182949], "pop" : 1240, "state" : "MA" }
{ "_id" : "01010", "city" : "BRIMFIELD", "loc" : [-72.188455, 42.116543], "pop" : 3706, "state" : "MA" }
{ "_id" : "01011", "city" : "CHESTER", "loc" : [-72.988761, 42.279421], "pop" : 1688, "state" : "MA" }

to import this data-set to the database named "test" and collection named "zips"

C:\Users\yc03ak1>mongoimport --db test --collection "zips" --drop --type json --host "localhost:47019" --file "c:\Users\yc03ak1\Desktop\zips.json"

--db : name of the database where data is to be imported to

--collection: name of the collection in the database where data is to be improted

--drop : drops the collection first before importing

--type : document type which needs to be imported. default JSON

--host : mongodb host and port on which data is to be imported.   --file : path where the json file is output :

2016-08-10T20:10:50.159-0700   connected to: localhost:47019

2016-08-10T20:10:50.163-0700	dropping: test.zips		
2016-08-10T20:10:53.155-0700	[###############........] test.zips	2.1	MB/3.0 MB (68.5%)
2016-08-10T20:10:56.150-0700	[#######################] test.zips	3.0	MB/3.0 MB (100.0%)
2016-08-10T20:10:57.819-0700	[#######################] test.zips	3.0	MB/3.0 MB (100.0%)
2016-08-10T20:10:57.821-0700	imported 29353 documents		

Section 14.4: mongoimport with CSV

Sample test dataset CSV file stored at the location c:\Users\yc03ak1\Desktop\testing.csv

_id	city	Loc	pop	state	
1	A	[10.0, 20.0]	2222	PQE	
2	E	[10.1, 20.1]	22122	RW	
3	C	[10.2, 20.0]	255222	RWE	
4	D	[10.3, 20.3]	226622	SFDS	
5	E	[10.4, 20.0]	222122	FDS	

to import this data-set to the database named "test" and collection named "sample"

C:\Users\yc03ak1>mongoimport --db test --collection "sample" --drop --type csv --headerline --host "localhost:47019" --file "c:\Users\yc03ak1\Desktop\testing.csv"

--headerline : use the first line of the csv file as the fields for the json document

output :

2016-08-10T20:25:48.572-0700	connected to: localhost:47019
2016-08-10T20:25:48.576-0700	dropping: test.sample
2016-08-10T20:25:49.109-0700	imported 5 documents

OR

C:\Users\yc03ak1>mongoimport --db test --collection "sample" --drop --type csv --fields _id,city,loc,pop,state --host "localhost:47019" --file "c:\Users\yc03ak1\Desktop\testing.csv"

--fields : comma separated list of fields which needs to be imported in the json document. Output:

2016-08-10T20:26:48.978-0700	connected to: localhost:47019
2016-08-10T20:26:48.982-0700	dropping: test.sample
2016-08-10T20:26:49.611-0700	imported 6 documents

Chapter 15:
Upgrading MongoDB version

How to update the version of MongoDB on your machine on di erent platforms and versions.

Section 15.1: Upgrading to 4.0 on Ubuntu 16.04 using apt

You must have 3.2 and later version to be able to upgrade to 4.0 This example assumes you are using apt.

sudo service mongod stop

sudo apt-key adv --keyserver hkp://keyserver.ubuntu.com:80 --recv 0C49F3730359A14518585931BC711F9BA15703C6

echo "deb [arch=amd64,arm64] http://repo.mongodb.org/apt/ubuntu xenial/mongodb-org/4.0 multiverse" | **sudo tee** /etc/apt/sources.list.d/mongodb-org-4.0.list

sudo apt-get update

sudo apt-get upgrade

sudo service mongod **start**

Ensure the new version is running with mongo. The shell will print out the MongoDB server version that should be 4.0 now.

Chapter 16:
MongoDB GridFS, Querying Capped Collection, Sequence

GridFS is the MongoDB specification for storing and retrieving large files such as images, audio files, video files, etc. It is kind of a file system to store files but its data is stored within MongoDB collections. GridFS has the capability to store files even greater than its document size limit of 16MB.
GridFS divides a file into chunks and stores each chunk of data in a separate document, each of maximum size 255k.
GridFS by default uses two collections **fs.files** and **fs.chunks** to store the file's metadata and the chunks. Each chunk is identified by its unique _id ObjectId field. The fs.files serves as a parent document. The **files_id** field in the fs.chunks document links the chunk to its parent.
Following is a sample document of fs.files collection -

```
{
  "filename": "test.txt",
  "chunkSize": NumberInt(261120),
  "uploadDate": ISODate("2014-04-13T11:32:33.557Z"),
  "md5": "7b762939321e146569b07f72c62cca4f",
  "length": NumberInt(646)
}
```

The document specifies the file name, chunk size, uploaded date, and length.
Following is a sample document of fs.chunks document -

```
{
  "files_id": ObjectId("534a75d19f54bfec8a2fe44b"),
  "n": NumberInt(0),
  "data": "Mongo Binary Data"
}
```

Adding Files to GridFS
Now, we will store an mp3 file using GridFS using the **put** command. For this, we will use the **mongofiles.exe** utility present in the bin folder of the MongoDB installation folder.
Open your command prompt, navigate to the mongofiles.exe in the bin folder of MongoDB installation folder and type the following code -

```
>mongofiles.exe -d gridfs put song.mp3
```

Here, **gridfs** is the name of the database in which the file will be stored. If the database is not present, MongoDB will automatically create a new document on the fly. Song.mp3 is the name of the file uploaded. To see the file's document in database, you can use find query -

```
>db.fs.files.find()
```

The above command returned the following document -

```
{
  _id: ObjectId('534a811bf8b4aa4d33fdf94d'),
  filename: "song.mp3",
  chunkSize: 261120,
  uploadDate: new Date(1397391643474), md5: "e4f53379c909f7bed2e9d631e15c1c41",
  length: 10401959
}
```

We can also see all the chunks present in fs.chunks collection related to the stored file with the following code, using the document id returned in the previous query -

```
>db.fs.chunks.find({files_id:ObjectId('534a811bf8b4aa4d33fdf94d')})
```

In my case, the query returned 40 documents meaning that the whole mp3 document was divided in 40 chunks of data.

MongoDB - Capped Collections

Capped collections are fixed-size circular collections that follow the insertion order to support high performance for create, read, and delete operations. By circular, it means that when the fixed size allocated to

75

the collection is exhausted, it will start deleting the oldest document in the collection without providing any explicit commands.

Capped collections restrict updates to the documents if the update results in increased document size. Since capped collections store documents in the order of the disk storage, it ensures that the document size does not increase the size allocated on the disk. Capped collections are best for storing log information, cache data, or any other high volume data.

Creating Capped Collection

To create a capped collection, we use the normal createCollection command but with **capped** option as **true** and specifying the maximum size of collection in bytes.

```
>db.createCollection("cappedLogCollection",{capped:true,size:10000})
```

In addition to collection size, we can also limit the number of documents in the collection using the **max** parameter −

```
>db.createCollection("cappedLogCollection",{capped:true,size:10000,max:1000})
```

If you want to check whether a collection is capped or not, use the following **isCapped** command −

```
>db.cappedLogCollection.isCapped()
```

If there is an existing collection which you are planning to convert to capped, you can do it with the following code −

```
>db.runCommand({"convertToCapped":"posts",size:10000})
```

This code would convert our existing collection **posts** to a capped collection.

Querying Capped Collection

By default, a find query on a capped collection will display results in insertion order. But if you want the documents to be retrieved in reverse order, use the **sort** command as shown in the following code −

```
>db.cappedLogCollection.find().sort({$natural:-1})
```

There are few other important points regarding capped collections worth knowing −

- We cannot delete documents from a capped collection.
- There are no default indexes present in a capped collection, not even on _id field.
- While inserting a new document, MongoDB does not have to actually look for a place to accommodate new document on the disk. It can blindly insert the new document at the tail of the collection. This makes insert operations in capped collections very fast.
- Similarly, while reading documents MongoDB returns the documents in the same order as present on disk. This makes the read operation very fast.

Auto-Increment Sequence

MongoDB does not have out-of-the-box auto-increment functionality, like SQL databases. By default, it uses the 12-byte ObjectId for the **_id** field as the primary key to uniquely identify the documents. However, there may be scenarios where we may want the _id field to have some auto-incremented value other than the ObjectId.

Since this is not a default feature in MongoDB, we will programmatically achieve this functionality by using a **counters** collection as suggested by the MongoDB documentation.

Using Counter Collection

Consider the following **products** document. We want the _id field to be an **auto-incremented integer sequence** starting from 1,2,3,4 upto n.

```
{
  "_id":1,
  "product_name": "Apple iPhone",
  "category": "mobiles"
}
```

For this, create a **counters** collection, which will keep track of the last sequence value for all the sequence fields.

```
>db.createCollection("counters")
```

Now, we will insert the following document in the counters collection with **productid** as its key −

```
{
  "_id":"productid",
```

```
"sequence_value": 0
}
```
The field **sequence_value** keeps track of the last value of the sequence.
Use the following code to insert this sequence document in the counters collection -
```
>db.counters.insert({_id:"productid",sequence_value:0})
```

References

1. *Awesome! MongoDB in a nutshell. —Hardy Ferentschik, Red Hat*

2. *Excellent. Many practical examples. —Curtis Miller, Flatterline*

3. *Not only the how, but also the why. —Philip Hallstrom, PJKH*

4. *Has a developer-centric flavor—an excellent reference. —Rick Wagner, Red Hat*

5. *MongoDB: The Definitive Guide by Kristina Chodorow*

6. *The Little MongoDB Book by Karl Seguin*

7. *MongoDB in Action by Kyle Banker*

8. *MongoDB Applied Design Patterns by Rick Copeland*

9. **The Definitive Guide to MongoDB by Eelco Plugge**

10. **Scaling MongoDB by Kristina Chodorow**

Printed in Great Britain
by Amazon